Praise for 'Redemptive family'

Howard Webb has done it! His thoughtful, transparent, and courageous book addresses the question too many of us have had but were too afraid to ask: Why does my church experience often leave me longing for something so much more? Howard not only answers this question but provides us with a biblical prescription and some practical therapy to help us rediscover God's original intention for His Church. I dare you to read it for your sake and your church's sake!

Doug Pollock
Author of God Space / GodsGPS.com

Redemptive Family concisely walks a Christian through what needs to change in their church to be a missional community. Be prepared to have your comfortable church assumptions challenged and the courage to take Howard's advice from his forty years of experience reaching people for Jesus. Read this book with other like-minded Christians and be ready for God to lead you.

Justin O'Malley
National Director, Tandem Ministries

I started reading this book having experienced church@onetwosix. It's a place that's inclusive, a place where you can be safely vulnerable. It's a place that mirrors real life with no pretence. There's a sense of family around the dinner table. It's awesome and obviously caring. Now that I've read this book, I am compelled to take personal action. There is so much within the covers of this book that reinforces what we at mainly music are about. Thank you, Howard. We will be referring many to its message.

Jo Hood
CEO, mainly music International

I love Howard's vision for the church. This book, I hope, is the start of a revolution of how we should be thinking, dreaming, and envisioning what it could be. If you are passionate about the church, looking to disciple people and see your church become more of a family that reaches out together, then start reading because you are not going to be able to put this book down!

Jono Hesp
National Director, Alpha New Zealand 2011-2017

I love how this book reminds the WHOLE Church—you, me and everyone else who identifies as living in Christ—that we are all called to play a vital part in the mission of God. *Redemptive Family* describes how one small local church is making this a reality for their WHOLE church whānau in their corner of the world. The simplicity of the principles in this book make them profoundly uncomfortable to ignore—and they just might change the world!

Aimee Mai
Chief Executive, Christians Against Poverty NZ

Redemptive
family

How church as a family,
rooted in a place, lies at the
heart of God's mission

Howard Webb

Torn Curtain Publishing
Wellington, New Zealand
www.torncurtainpublishing.com

ISBN Softcover 978-0-473-53412-7
ISBN Kindle 978-0-473-53414-1
ISBN PDF 978-0-473-53415-8

Cover photo credit: Jaakko Blomberg. Used with permission.

A catalogue record for this book is available from the National Library of New Zealand.

Redemptive
family

How church as a family,
rooted in a place, lies at the
heart of God's mission

Foreword

The most valuable books are written by people with a rich diversity of experience in their particular field. Howard Webb is one of those people. He is no mere missional theorist. Rather, along with his critical mind and avid hunger to read and grow, he brings to this work years of missional experience from university ministries, church ministry, and more recently, church planting. Moreover, Howard has excellent literary skills that make this book engaging and interesting from start to finish.

In an age where the Western church struggles to find its missional edge, Howard is not afraid to challenge the status quo. Yet he does so in a winsome manner that is faithful to the Scriptures. This makes his book a must-read for those of us in Western contexts grappling with the same old same old of church life, insipid discipleship, and a lack of missional zeal and effectiveness. His ideas are biblical and remarkably simple, showing how the model of church as family lies at the centre of God's vision of a new humanity. His approach declericalises church planting, church life, and sharing the faith in a way that gives hope to those jaded by religion. His writing reflects his warmth and zeal for making disciples who make disciples.

It has been a privilege to walk with Howard on this journey as a book coach, often finding myself the student rediscovering the simple wonder of God's missional agenda. I do hope this book gets into the hands of as many missioners and church leaders as possible. I encourage you to read it and pass it on, as we should the Gospel. I believe God will use it to see new churches planted, to renew existing ones, and raise a generation of faithful disciples who God will use to rekindle the faith in New Zealand and beyond.

Rev. Dr. Mark J. Keown
Senior Lecturer in New Testament
Laidlaw College

Author's Note

I have used the term 'missioner' in this book to describe those who gather as part of a church family on a mission. If we refer to ourselves only as 'church-goers' or 'congregants,' this implies that our purpose is simply to congregate. Describing ourselves as 'worshippers' is better—yet our purpose is greater even than that. We need a label that reminds us that we are on a mission from God.

The word 'missioners' is an archaic word that used to simply mean 'missionary,' and although it has fallen out of our modern vocabulary, there is much value in recycling it and once again putting it to good use.

* * *

All Scripture references are taken from the New Living Translation (NLT), the version we have adopted at our church plant in Point Chevalier, New Zealand, a missional family we simply refer to as *church@onetwosix*.

Acknowledgements

I wish to make special mention of those who helped make this book possible: Lynette, my wife, for her proofreading and wise counsel and for giving me the space to write; Bruce Edmonds, friend and colleague at *Love Your Neighbour*, for his proofreading, optimism and big-picture thinking; Justin O'Malley, National Director of Tandem Ministries, for his enthusiastic encouragement; Karl Udy and Matt Coyle, my *Tandem* colleagues, for sending material my way they knew would be helpful; Dr. Mark Keown of Laidlaw College for being my book-writing coach; my children Wesley, Dylan and Catherine for their thoughtful feedback and design skills; Evan and Katherine Barker, Kaylynn Mills and Jo Hood for their proofreading and suggestions; and Anya McKee of Torn Curtain Publishing for all her work in getting this book to print.

I also want to express my appreciation for the folks at *church@onetwosix* for being the proof of the pudding, with special mention of co-leaders Lynette, Bruce and Vicky Edmonds, and Murray and Karen Cottle.

My heartfelt thanks to all of you!

Howard Webb
July 2020

Contents

Introduction

We all know the model for 'Sunday church' well. Throughout the week a few people have worked hard to produce the event that is about to unfold. The preacher, worship team, and kids church leaders have all come prepared for their role in the programme. The goal is to create a worshipful atmosphere through singing and corporate prayer in order to prepare hearts for the lesson or word of exhortation from Scripture that follows. We will then probably sing again, close in prayer, and head out to the foyer for a cup of tea and fellowship.

Most of the congregation will come with nothing much to contribute, but with a pleasant expectation of a familiar ritual. Sundays are a bit like dinner—what will be on the menu today? We like a bit of variety on the plate, but we also know we can count on getting meat and three veg. With Sunday church consumed, we feel the afterglow. We will come back next Sunday ready to do it all over again.

There is much about 'regular' church that is good and valuable, yet there remains something unsatisfactory about this picture. Church leaders sense it and so do those who sit in the pew. It's an experience that soothes, rather than transforms. It's more about comfort than challenge. It's slippers, not work boots. Here is the dilemma we face in the church in New Zealand and throughout the West. Do we keep tweaking what we have, hoping for better results? Or do we try something new?

A 2019 cartoon strip by 'Dilbert' creator, Scott Adams, captures the moment perfectly. In it, Alice is talking to the pointy-haired boss. 'One option,' she says, 'is to use the method that has never once worked, but we think we know how to make it work next time. The other option is to try something new that we can't be sure will work. It's almost as if leadership is nothing but guessing.'

Alice's boss, who has been standing with his coffee mug halfway to his mouth, replies, 'Let's change the subject.'

The evidence tells us that our current model of church is not very good at producing what we would most like to see—radically transformed lives. Yet there are plenty of reasons why we may choose to change the subject and press on with our unsatisfactory model rather than ask hard questions of the model itself.

For most of us, this way of doing church is all we have ever experienced. Years (perhaps generations) of investment in buildings and programmes have been made with the current model in mind. Embedded also is our funding model; if we change how we do church, how will we pay for it all? We would have to reshape the expectations of our congregation, and no one likes change. And what about our faithful church staff? The value and meaning of their life work are bound up in this time-honoured way of doing church. Changing the model would require a new narrative around purpose and what we will call success. In short, doing things differently would take a lot of courage and would likely make a lot of people unhappy.

For too long we have been giving people what they want instead of what they need. Our people may think they want an engaging experience of church without demands or accountability because they are such busy people. Many churches have tacitly agreed to play by these rules. They polish the Sunday service to attract attenders, and delegate all the work to staff teams or small groups of volunteers so as not to burden the 'regulars.' The result is that 'the regulars' grow spiritually weak. They are not exercising faith or seeing God move. By trying to do all we can to keep people in church, we paradoxically create an environment that risks having them drift away from church and from God.

What our people really need is the exact opposite, and deep down we know it. If they are to become disciples who walk in the power of the Spirit, demonstrate the transformational power of the Gospel in their lives, and are willing to pay any price to follow Jesus, they need a model of church that supports and encourages them to become part of God's redemptive story.

They need a church that meets their deep need for community, while providing opportunity to find their own purpose within the bigger purpose of the church family. Most importantly, they need a church that models discipleship and expects them to participate and grow spiritually.

It turns out that this alternative model of church already has an impressive track record. It is the picture of church that we find throughout the New Testament—a church that is not primarily a ritual-keeping institution, but *a family on a mission together.*

I have experienced first-hand the joy of being part of exactly that sort of faith community. It was deeply transformative of my life and of many others besides. It was this experience that prompted my wife Lynette and me to devote our lives full-time to faith-based ministry twenty-five years ago. And it is an experience I would dearly love to share with church leaders who are wrestling with the reality of a church that has grown pale and wan and is in need of change.

The bad news is that church as family can't simply be grafted onto our regular model of 'Sunday church.' Choosing to be a family on a mission requires rethinking how we do church from the ground up. For instance, a significant part of our time together will need to be spent in deepening relationships, a family non-negotiable.

Regular 'Sunday church' promises relationship and mutuality, but in reality offers only crumbs. Time on Sunday is given to listening to preachers and worship leaders, while most of the congregation sit passively, unable to meaningfully communicate with the person beside them without being rude. Precious few get the chance to have a deep conversation before or after the church service about the things that matter most, and even fewer get to exercise their spiritual gifts when church is gathered.

By contrast, growing relationships is at the heart of both family and mission, therefore a church family on a mission together will make time for relationships. It is only through taking time that we get to know, trust, and love each other. This is what makes us authentic. This is where giftings have a chance to shine through. And this is what will stand out to our seeking friends when we invite them to join us at the family table.

The good news is that reshaping our church to be a family on a mission together does us and our people so much good. It simplifies church and makes it more real. It is highly participatory and gets leaders off the treadmill of having to provide yet another slick programme on Sunday. The gathering itself becomes part of our mission, rather than 'time out' from ordinary life. If you are a leader who has grown tired of 'playing the game,' this vision of church will reignite your passion for ministry.

Perhaps you are thinking of branching out and starting something new. That is fantastic. Multiplying church families is central to God's plan for reaching the world. Planting churches with this simple DNA can be done by anybody in any context, as we will discover together.

At some point, however, we all have to face the quandary posed by Alice. Will we stick with the old model, determined to make it work, or will we risk doing something new even though we cannot be certain of the outcome? I hope to persuade you that the risk is worth it.

1
Out of the Kettle

You have probably heard the illustration of the frog in a kettle. As the story goes, if you throw a frog into boiling water it will immediately jump out, but if you place it in a pot of cold water and warm it slowly, it will gradually be lulled into a stupor, miss the danger signals, and ultimately be boiled to death. True or not, let's go with the metaphor for a moment.

I am on the boundary of baby-boomer and Gen X—the television series, *The Wonder Years* could have been about my childhood—and as I reflect on my experience of growing up in church, I note how different it was to the church my children were raised in a generation later. The water temperature had changed.

For one thing, we grew up attending church a lot more. Sunday School was followed by the morning service, then we returned that evening for yet more time in church. After the evening service, we would frequently go to someone's home for a hot drink and more chorus-singing. Attending a mid-week Bible study (usually delivered as a monologue) was expected of everyone. As teenagers we had it lucky; we would cram into a lounge for a Bible study on a 'relevant' topic. Our discussions were animated and engaging. On Friday nights we had 'youth night,' the highlight of our week.

Still, this was no 'golden age' of the church. We had reason to be concerned about the tendency of being simply a social club and not reaching our world. Our church-inspired events were not slick, but sometimes they were boring and occasionally even cringe-worthy. The pews were hard and uncomfortable. You dressed up for church because it was a solemn occasion and you wanted to show respect for God—yet the event itself was low-key and utterly predictable.

These church events were, nevertheless, opportunities to participate in community. They were the telegraph poles between which we strung our lives. We knew the inside of each other's houses because we socialised—a lot—in a much simpler world. We were in church as much for each other as for any spiritual reason, yet along the way we heard and absorbed the Gospel. Despite all the shortcomings of church, we were becoming biblically literate, and we shared enough of life together that we helped form each other's worldview. Church was like a home-knitted woollen jumper, ill-fitting and scratchy, but the community woven through it kept you warm.

The world has shifted since my early days in church however, and many books have been written on the subject. Church is no longer mainstream in our culture, and attendance does not confer respectability. Full-time homemakers with flexible schedules have mostly joined the workforce and are no longer available to serve as the volunteer help and social glue that held so much extramural church activity together. Shopping, sports, the internet, and a myriad of increasingly sophisticated entertainment options now compete with church on Sundays. And, in many ways, the digital age has brought with it a hyper-individualism and a shift away from in-person social interaction.

If we had only seen the change coming and appreciated how big it would be, we may have stopped to reflect on whether we needed to replace our tired and worn model of church for a new one. Instead, we kept patching up the old model of Sunday church, making piecemeal accommodations to the societal changes tugging at us. We focused on making the jumper less scratchy, but lost sight of what the jumper is for; we have forgotten God's purpose in establishing His church on earth in the first place.

Faced with the pressure of busyness and the fragmentation of modern life, we stopped attending two services on a Sunday, a pattern that has led most churches to move to a single service (which may be repeated for multiple audiences). Our youth are generally sent out from this single service to attend their own age-specific programme.

Very few of us also connect through the rest of the week. Statistics are lacking for New Zealand, but in America, the proportion of a congregation who also participate in a home-based small group is reported to have a ceiling of about 35%.[i] In many churches I know of, it is less than that. Churches are becoming relationally poor; the bedrock of community on which our model of 'doing church' was founded has been eroded away. We just don't know each other like we used to.

We focused on making the jumper less scratchy, but lost sight of what the jumper is for

As our church-led circles of interaction have contracted, we have come to hang everything on that precious Sunday service as our flagship event. We have relaxed our dress code, done away with the 'hymn-and-a-thing' sandwich and ramped up our worship with bands and stage lighting. We have taken the work once done by volunteers and included it in the job description for paid professional staff.

Church has never been more relaxed, entertaining, or professionally produced yet despite all the good vibes the overall number of church attenders continues to fall, with the drop-out rate increasing for each successive generation. If Bible reading is an indicator of spiritual growth, it should concern us that perhaps only 9% of Christian millennials read Scripture daily, and only 13% even read it every week.[ii]

We need to face up to the fact that our regular model of doing church isn't working. What we are seeing are the natural consequences of a systemic failure to make disciples. Taken alone, what we typically do on Sunday mornings in our Western model of church has always been incapable of making disciples, yet the Sunday service is the only experience of church that most of our people now get. Church may no longer be ill-fitting and scratchy—it has been re-made into a soft, tailored garment that is a delight to put on—but it has also become too thin to keep out the cold.

Perhaps you have seen the picture floating around the internet of the disciples sitting in rows of desks out in the fields, with Jesus at the whiteboard 'discipling' them. We instantly get what the picture is trying to convey—that this is not an effective path to discipleship.

Discipleship happens when we see behaviours and attitudes and acts of faith modelled for us and are then held accountable for practising them ourselves. It simply does not happen in a space designed to meet our personal needs whilst keeping us comfortably anonymous. The Western church has replaced 'making disciples' with a form of 'Christianity-lite,' catering to busy, distracted people, but also asking and expecting less and less of them—and it is slowly killing the church.

Our life's purpose is no longer about serving our own dreams and plans; rather, it is about helping to bring all things under the lordship of Christ

A vital faith, however, requires that we make the costly commitment to lay down our lives in the service of Jesus, and then ask our faith community to hold us accountable for doing so. Our life's purpose is no longer about serving our own dreams and plans; rather, it is about helping to bring all things under the lordship of Christ by faith-stretching means. True church is where we gather with like-minded brothers and sisters in the unity and power of the Spirit to experience the encouragement, exhortation, discipline and equipping we need to be a disciple—and it is the place where we get to use our spiritual gifts to the full as we minister into the lives of others.

We need to stop asking, 'What can we achieve without changing how we do church or making more demands on our congregation?' When we only ever ask this too-small and too-safe question, we doom ourselves to achieving less and less until we are simply not being church anymore. We are the frog slowly succumbing as the water temperature rises.

The true question is, 'What must we do to be successful as God's church on earth?' This question is bold, challenging, and costly, but it leads to hope and life; it is the frog jumping out of the kettle. Frogs don't belong in kettles! We do not need to keep the kettle, *or* to regulate the temperature. The church needs to cast aside the constraints of a model that is not working and find a new way to be church—one that gets us back to our original purpose.

WHAT WILL WE CALL SUCCESS?

Without a vision of what we want or of what success might look like, we cannot begin taking steps towards it. A different future must always begin in our imagination. Let your mind's eye picture what your church might look like five years from now. Does the future you dream of look different to how it is today?

I do not dream of greater excellence in our Sunday programme. Rather, I dream of greater intimacy and connection with my church family. I see people with radiant faces eagerly waiting to tell their story of what God has just done for them. Others are bursting to share the fresh insights they have discovered in Scripture. Some are weeping with repentance and joy because they really have experienced the Gospel as good news. I see people loving each other who can't wait to be together again—and who bring their friends to experience it too. I dream of church that sees the world through the eyes of Jesus and cares about the things that He also cares about.

> I see people loving each other who can't wait to be together again

This may sound too good to be true, but it was a lived reality for the early church. In Acts 2, we find ordinary, anxious believers brought out of hiding, transformed by the Holy Spirit, and caught up into an unstoppable movement.

Let's pick up the narrative from verse 42:

> *All the believers devoted themselves to the apostles' teaching, and to fellowship, and to sharing in meals (including the Lord's Supper), and to prayer. A deep sense of awe came over them all, and the apostles performed many miraculous signs and wonders.*

And all the believers met together in one place and shared everything they had. They sold their property and possessions and shared the money with those in need. They worshipped together at the Temple each day, met in homes for the Lord's Supper, and shared their meals with great joy and generosity—all the while praising God and enjoying the goodwill of all the people.

And each day the Lord added to their fellowship those who were being saved (Acts 2:42-47).

Does this account of passionate Christian living stir your heart? Perhaps, like me, you long to be swept up into an authentic spiritual movement like that.

Spiritual movements are a bit wild and messy. They are organic and highly relational environments where faith is exercised and grown through being validated. Fixed structures and systems struggle to keep up—as we discover later in Acts 6.

Spiritual movements also excite us because we sense that being part of one would lead to our own personal transformation. Being part of a movement centres our whole existence. It becomes the most important thing. Anyone who gets close enough can feel it. As we get caught up in what God is doing, we discover our purpose and gain God's Kingdom perspective.

Let me tell you about my own experience of moving from 'regular' church to being part of a spiritual movement and why I think that church should not settle for anything less.

My off-ramp to missional community

I grew up in a Christian home, had a personal faith, and regularly attended a good church that preached the Gospel message. Yet I had never experienced the joy, the intensity or deep bonding that comes with being connected to a group of like-minded people all committed to a mission.

It was my involvement as a student with Campus Crusade for Christ (now called 'Cru') in the early 1980's that profoundly influenced the rest of my life.

Through this movement on the University of the Witwatersrand campus in Johannesburg, South Africa, I made many lifelong friends—including my best friend, my wife Lynette. It is not altogether surprising that, years later, we seized the opportunity to work for the organisation in New Zealand (now Tandem Ministries) and have continued to serve in that ministry for twenty-five years.

Having reflected on what made my campus experience so spiritually vibrant and on the implications for the church, I have come to believe that our 'secret sauce' had little to do with the unique campus environment and a lot to do with universal principles of spiritual movement-building which the declining Western church must also embrace or risk fading away.

It was an experience of church family on mission

As students on campus, we were often told that what we were doing was not 'church' and was not a substitute for church. However, from the inside, it looked and felt very much like a local 'campus-church.'

It is true that our narrow focus on evangelism did not reflect the breadth of God's mission for the church, but we did what every church does—we read Scripture, we prayed, we sang, and we received teaching. We may not have shared the Lord's Supper, but we did eat prodigious amounts of pizza

> I have come to believe that our 'secret sauce' had little to do with the unique campus environment and a lot to do with universal principles of spiritual movement-building

together with glad and sincere hearts! Those with vehicles crammed them full whenever we went anywhere together. We gave each other dating advice. We rejoiced together about those coming into the Kingdom, and there was a clear pathway for quickly assimilating new believers.

Even baptisms happened, if somewhat off the record. After teaching my discipleship group about baptism, John (a new believer) declared that he would like to be baptised. A group of us went down to the swimming pool at our hall of residence early in the morning so as not to be in the public eye. As I stood in the freezing cold water with John, our friend Alan (who was warmly bundled up beside the pool) prayed for him. And prayed. And prayed! John and I nearly died of hypothermia that morning. But glancing around at the friends who had gathered to witness the occasion, I was struck by the fact that we were far more than friends—we had become family.

> I was struck by the fact that we were far more than friends; we had become family

In my four active years as a student on campus, our numbers grew from around seventy to nearly three hundred—and bear in mind that our graduating students were leaving campus each year! I understand that these numbers may seem modest compared to other stories of growth based on attendance figures. But these students were missioners, not attenders. We had meetings of course, but our central activity was not a great gathering of the faithful. Mission was the main event, and everyone who was part of the movement was a participant.

There was a clear pathway to success

One of the hallmarks of our campus movement was that there was clarity about *what* the goal was, we were all on board regarding *why* we were doing it, and we all understood exactly *how* we would do it.

Through appointments or by meeting up on campus, we would seek to have a spiritual conversation with students, leading them through a booklet outlining the Gospel. If they showed an interest, we would follow them up. If they prayed to receive Christ, we did follow-up Bible study with them to cement their commitment and make sure they had assurance of salvation.

We then did our best to include these students in a group with others who were also starting out on their faith journey. They would be invited to large group events and camps. From an early stage, they would be challenged to tag along on an evangelism appointment and 'get their feet wet.' As they progressed, we would invite them to begin leading others, teaching them that if they were to lead, they only needed to be one step ahead! Everyone was in a discipleship group, and the goal was that everyone would also lead a group of their own in a chain of discipleship.

We received on-the-job training in how to use certain tools and materials (such as the evangelism booklet and follow-up materials) and in other necessary skills, such as the dynamics of leading a small group. If a person was saved on campus and faithfully committed to the process, after two years they would be a Christian leader, well-grounded in the basics of the faith with those they had intentionally discipled already making disciples of their own.

We had mentoring and accountability

Our leaders modelled 'doing evangelism' and leading a small group for us and encouraged us to give it go. First, they modelled what we were to do. Then they moved to letting us take the lead with them assisting us. Eventually, they were just watching us and giving feedback. Soon we found that we were the leaders modelling mission for others. We knew we could always go to our leaders for advice and encouragement because they had been there themselves. Through the discipleship groups, we were also held accountable for fulfilling our evangelistic mission.

We worked with the rhythms of a shared place

The campus was our shared place and its boundaries gave our mission scope. We wanted to reach the campus for Christ, and that concrete objective helped us decide what we would do to achieve our goal. Limiting our scope to our campus (rather than aiming to save the whole world) helped us measure success; the enthusiasm and faith-building that flowed from having evidence of that success helped the movement grow.

As students, we had familiar and predictable rhythms that we worked with. Back in the day, there was a twenty-minute mid-morning tea break. Our favourite place to hang out together was on the steps of the Great Hall—we would go there to connect with the campus ministry crowd whenever we could. We also knew where to go to find students who might be willing to go through the Gospel outline with us. We would go to the cafeteria, to those eating lunch by the pool, or to students sitting on the lawns or on the low stone walls around campus. The nooks and crannies and peculiarities of our campus were known to us, and we worked with them. The shape of the campus shaped us and our mission.

We did mission together

We called it 'personal evangelism' back then, but I see now that the real driver behind our effectiveness on campus was the fact that we did it together. By going together, we were bolder. We complemented each other's strengths. We could debrief with each other about an experience we had just had.

> We could not have become a self-perpetuating spiritual movement without the exhilaration of tasting success and having fun along the way

Importantly, modelling and accountability were built in. It was a faith-stretching adventure that bonded us as fellow missioners precisely because it was a little bit scary.

The most important dynamic though, is easily overlooked—we were having fun together! We could never have become a self-perpetuating spiritual movement without the exhilaration of tasting success and having fun along the way.

Hard landings

Trying to integrate back into my old home church after my years on campus wasn't easy. Despite the debt of gratitude I owed my church for the work of spiritual formation I had benefitted from in my growing-up years, I now had a hole they couldn't fill. Church did not feel like a movement and it was simply not structured for the outcomes we had seen on campus. Of course, the people in my church had not been on my journey, nor had my experiences. Besides, I was so familiar with the long-established rhythms of my church that they seemed unchangeable to me. I lacked the imagination to see how I could make a difference, and so I said and did very little about it.

After my time on campus, I took a job at the city council—an environment far less conducive to the style of personal ministry I was used to. My days were now structured around getting work done rather than socialising. The lunch break was a chance to escape into the city for shopping or to buy lunch. Everyone worked to their own daily rhythm of balancing personal time, family, and work. The reality of hierarchical relationships of authority and the pressure to succeed (or just stay out of trouble!) resulted in many of my work relationships being perfunctory at best. I tried using the Gospel booklet a few times, but without the desired response. Soon, workmates began avoiding me in the corridors. To be effective as a Christian in the workplace I really needed my church's help. I now have some ideas about how I could have brought my church friends and my work friends together for the sake of the Kingdom, but then I did not. In my mind, church and work were two separate circles.

After moving into an apartment, I imagined that I could somehow reach out to my life-hardened neighbours with the Gospel, but as a young single guy still wet behind the ears, I was at a loss to know how to go about it. A natural introvert, I just couldn't find the intersection points between my life and theirs. Once again, I really needed my church's help. Had I thought about it, I knew people in my home church whose lives did have the necessary intersection points, and I could have been the matchmaker. Sadly, this option never occurred to me. While on campus I had been buoyed by our shared mission, but I now felt dislocated and guilty for being so evangelistically ineffective on my own.

But something else was happening too—the busyness of life. My time with the Lord was starting to get squeezed. I was in love and getting married. What can compete with that? I was immersed in my new legal career, and work occupied a great deal of headspace. My spiritual fervour slowly waned.

I stayed in church, thanks largely to my deep roots in my home church. My church was filled with God-fearing believers of long acquaintance that I loved dearly, and we practised church no differently from any other church I knew of. So I stayed and settled back down. Later, Lynette and I were married in that church. I served as a deacon and led a homegroup for many years while Lynette taught Sunday School and played the piano for services. It was the church we left when we emigrated to New Zealand, and they have faithfully supported us as missionaries all these years. It was and remains a good church.

These days our campus ministry in New Zealand, Student Life, is asking the question, 'What happens after campus?' and is doing a good job of connecting students with existing local churches as they enter the post-campus world. We are training students in a range of tools and relational skills that are also effective in a non-campus environment. We actively pursue partnerships with campus-friendly churches, and personal engagement with a church has become one of our hallmarks of a healthy disciple. Our desire is to hook students into a regular church before they leave campus so that they already have a spiritual home where they belong once they leave. Despite all this, many of the graduates from our campus ministry find the transition to church frustrating and unfulfilling.

> Many of the graduates from our campus ministry find the transition to church frustrating and unfulfilling

Looking at church through different eyes

I invite you to look at typical Western church through the eyes of someone who has been part of a mission-centric movement on campus. The differences can be stark. For example:

Little time is spent on the enterprise. For most churchgoers, attendance is limited to an hour or two on Sunday mornings—and not even every Sunday. Those who attend a mid-week small group may spend a further hour or two in the company of other church members. Most of our campus graduates have been attending church and also making time for mission on campus. They now discover how little time is spent together productively as church.

How the church spends its time together is quite different. Most of the time spent in church consists of passive listening. On campus, time spent together is highly participatory and engaging of others. It requires contribution and involves a great deal of talking!

Focus is on a space. On campus, the space where gatherings happen is of little consequence. Any available room will do, because the purpose for gathering has nothing to do with the room. For church, on the other hand, the physical space is important. It needs to accommodate everyone at once. It must accommodate certain liturgical practices. It requires shaping and draping to best support the Sunday event. Almost everything the church does has the building as its nexus.

The central purpose is worship. The central Sunday event is worship through song, the preaching of the word and sacrament. The core purpose of Sunday church is not 'mission.'

Mission happens invisibly and provides no modelling. The regular missional programmes of the church involve only a few and happen at a time and place where they are not seen by most of the congregation. Consequently, there is no modelling of outreach for those outside the programme.

Mission is optional and without accountability. On the one hand, there is an understanding that everyone has a personal responsibility for mission in their everyday lives. On the other hand, there is no modelling or accountability for doing so. Outside of narrow mission-focussed programmes run by a few, participation by the wider congregation is encouraged through infrequent, one-off events. The purpose of these events is generally to make church seem relevant and fun rather than to introduce people to the Gospel. Engagement in these events is entirely optional and it is expected that the majority of the congregation will probably not participate.

Success is measured by attendance. This is related to the core purpose of church. If the core purpose was to see people come to Christ, one could measure outcomes, as we do on campus. But what appropriate measure is there for a worship service other than how many people come?

Can you feel the tension of someone returning to church life after being part of a successful mission movement on campus? The worship and the teaching may be great, and this is some consolation. What they miss, however, is the unifying sense of purpose found in shared mission.

The campus model of 'everyone being a missioner,' squares well with the picture of the church reflected in the New Testament. What do we do with the typical Western church model which seeks to attract attenders instead?

Lessons from campus

I understand that the context of university campus ministry is unique. University students are generally young, bright, healthy and energetic, and have more discretionary time at their disposal than they will ever enjoy again. Their lives are not complicated by work, marriage, children and other responsibilities.

The campus ministry is a three-year greenhouse for most who go through it, whereas church must come alongside people for a lifetime. It is clear that the church also must own a mission that is greater than evangelism alone. What we can learn from campus, however, is that the church needs to know its purpose, adopt a structure that will help it succeed, and measure outcomes if the church wishes to grow as a movement.

> The church needs to know its purpose, adopt a structure that will help it succeed, and measure outcomes if it wishes to grow as a movement

Our campus ministry defines their purpose through a little mantra that everyone in the movement is familiar with: 'Win, Build, Send.' When we are making disciples by winning people to Christ, building them up in their faith and then sending them to do likewise, we know we are fulfilling our purpose.

What outcomes should church be measuring to know that it is fulfilling its purpose? I suggest these:

- People in the church are laying down their lives for the sake of the Kingdom. They are growing in obedience and fruitfulness. This is what a true disciple looks like.

- The church practises being a family together. Their love and generosity towards each other is being noted by outsiders—it is a foretaste of the Kingdom. They choose to resolve conflict and extend forgiveness rather than walk away.

- The church's ministry of reconciliation to the world is bearing fruit in the community. They are befriending outsiders and wooing them to Jesus. They call on each other for help and encouragement. We see newcomers at the family table Sunday by Sunday.

My observation is that the typical Western church model is geared to making attenders comfortable and providing safety in anonymity. This seems like the wrong vehicle if the outcome we really want is to make disciples. Dallas Willard writes, 'Pastors need to redefine success. The popular model of success involves the ABC's—attendance, buildings, and cash. Instead of counting Christians, we need to weigh them.'[iii] Or in the words of A.W. Tozer, 'It is of far greater importance that we have better Christians than that we have more of them.'[iv]

This brings us to a crucial conclusion: *Churches that love their model more than how effectively they are making disciples, will die.* I believe that emphasising spiritual growth through engaging in mission together is the only way out of the kettle for the Western church.

Through the pages of this book I propose an alternative model for how we think about church and mission and how we spend our time together. This alternative model is built on the four key principles that I believe make the campus ministry so effective, and which we are implementing ourselves in our own church plant:

We are a family,

in a place,

on a mission,

together.

We will consider each point in turn in the chapters ahead. For now, let me conclude this chapter by responding to two arguments I have heard in defence of our present way of doing church.

IS CHANGE REALLY NECESSARY?

Here is some push-back I have received — and you may be thinking the same. If gathered worship, centred on preaching of the Scriptures and celebration of sacraments or ordinances stems from apostolic times, how can our Sunday pattern be 'wrong'? It's a fair enough question!

Aren't we doing church like it's always been done?

If we look back at our passage from Acts 2, worship, teaching, fellowship, prayer and the Lord's Supper are certainly all there. But it is a mistake to project the church we know back onto the church in Acts, thinking that church for them was just like ours.

The early disciples didn't go to church to practise these various elements as a formal 'identity ritual.' Rather, these practices had a quality that was life-giving and movement-sustaining. The church we read about met *every day*. It seems to have been a kind of rolling party, moving from home to home. This wasn't a ninety-minute obligation once a week, it was a way of life!

While these ordinances served the early church's purpose, we cannot discover their purpose just by looking at what they did. Christ was not building His church to practice the ordinances. Purpose is a *why* question. And the *why* of what they were doing was to learn to live out their new Spirit-filled life in Christ before the world. The *what* served the *why* and the result was that, 'Each day, the Lord added to their fellowship those who were being saved' (Acts 2:47).

Just ticking a ritual *'what'* box is not enough. Unless we are as clear as the early church was on the *why* of church, we are not doing church like it has always been done.

Isn't worship the heart of church?

Naturally, worship and mission should go hand in hand. When they do, God is glorified.

It is, however, possible to attempt to practice one without the other, in which case God is not glorified. Mission without a heart of worship becomes moralistic activism or loveless 'evangelism,' while worship without obedience to the call to mission is ultimately self-focused, even if God is in view. John 14:15 says, 'If you love me, obey my commandments.'

This does not mean that worship and mission have equal priority. For missiologist Chris Wright, 'mission' is much more than just a biblical theme; he asserts that the Bible is fundamentally about mission, that we are not just people who 'do missions' for God, but that

When we organize around anything other than mission, we create a system that can comfortably exist without mission

God Himself is a missionary God, and we have the privilege of being included in His mission. Mission is the overarching purpose of God and of His church.[v]

Every church must structure and organise itself for what it sees as its priority. Should our purpose, then, be worship . . . or mission?

The church performs several functions, all of which are important. Nevertheless, every organisation, including church, has an 'organising function'—it shapes itself to perform with the least amount of friction and fuss. Brian Knell points out that the function most Western churches have chosen to organise around, is worship. It dictates the shape and layout of our buildings, and how we budget our time on Sundays.[vi]

However, when we organise around anything other than mission, we create a system that can comfortably exist without mission. Church centred in worship or teaching does not need mission to feel complete. The importance of mission may be acknowledged, but it can feel like an intrusion.

When mission is the organising function of the church, we can't get comfortable. When we meet, we are confronted with the question of what we are doing in the world. Our testimonies of God at work prompts worship, praise and thanksgiving. The brokenness in the world — and ourselves — causes us to turn to God in supplication and dependency.

When faith is exercised, God answers, and faith grows. Worship is the natural response of the uncomfortable church centred in mission. When we put mission at the centre, everything else follows. We need to raise our sights to the overarching purpose of every Christian and hence the church.

In this regard I love the first article of the Westminster Shorter Catechism (and the fact that it is first!):

> **Q. What is the chief end of man?**
> A. Man's chief end is to glorify God, and to enjoy him forever.[vii]

God's eternal plan has always been to display His glory, not just through individuals, but through a body of believers that He calls His family. The church exists to glorify God. This singular purpose is behind everything we do.

The church is the unique instrument for bringing God such glory. According to the Bible, 'God's purpose in all this was to use the church to display his wisdom in its rich variety to all the unseen rulers and authorities in the heavenly places. This was his eternal plan, which he carried out through Christ Jesus our Lord' (Ephesians 3:10-11).

Glorifying God is much bigger than worship. We glorify God by our worshipful, obedient *doing*, which is mission.

These Scriptures make the point *(emphases mine):*

> I brought glory to you here on earth by **completing the work** you gave me to do (John 17:4).

> For **your generosity** to them and to all believers will prove that you are obedient to the Good News of Christ (2 Corinthians 9:13).

> In the same way, let your **good deeds** shine out for all to see, so that everyone will praise your heavenly Father (Matthew 5:16).

> When you **produce much fruit**, you are my true disciples. This brings great glory to my Father (John 15:8).

> So whether you eat or drink, or **whatever you do**, do it all for the glory of God (1 Corinthians 10:31).

MAKING OUR CHURCH A MISSION-CENTRED MOVEMENT

A mission-centred church can barely fail to become a growing movement.

A movement is:

a) a body of Spirit-filled believers, which

b) gathers others around an inspiring vision for how they might fulfil their mission in the world, and then

c) adopts support structures designed to help them succeed.

There is Spirit and there is structure. Both are needed. Without the work of the Spirit within, structure alone cannot produce results. It is like a power tool without a battery. But zeal without the right structure ends in frustration and disillusionment. It is like trying to build with the wrong tools—or without any tools at all.

Our church cannot both be transformed into a spiritual movement *and* continue doing the same things in the same way. As we cast a vision for a different future, we must be prepared to restructure to succeed. The challenge of this book is that, while its ideas are very simple, we must be prepared to do church differently.

Right now, your church and mine is either growing or dying. They are either like yeast working through a lump of dough, transforming the world around them, or they have lost their vital force. Faith is either being exercised and is growing, or it is withering on the vine. There can be no stasis in church.

Through the pages of this book, you will see that churches of any size, in any place, can restructure themselves into spiritual movements and save themselves from dying. I will share the story of our own church plant in Point Chevalier, Auckland, and the reflections of others who are grappling with how to grow the church in New Zealand. We do not begin by diving into mission, however. We must begin, like the Acts church did, by first becoming family. We will explore this in the next chapter.

[i] Joseph R. Myers, *The Search to Belong: Rethinking Intimacy, Community, and Small Groups* (Grand Rapids, Michigan: Zondervan, 2003).
[ii] "Digital Millennials and the Bible," www.biblesociety.org.uk/latest/news/digital-millennials-and-the-bible/.
[iii] Interview with Dallas Willard and Dieter Zander, www.dwillard.org/articles/individual/apprentices-the.
[iv] A. W. Tozer, *Tozer for the Christian Leader: A 365-Day Devotional* (Chicago: Moody; 2001).
[v] Christopher J. H. Wright. *The Mission of God: Unlocking the Bible's Grand Narrative* (Downers Grove, Il.: IVP, 2006).
[vi] Brian Knell. *The Heart of Church and Mission* (Nürnberg, Germany: VTR Publications, 2015).
[vii] "Shorter Catechism of the Assembly of Divines: The 1647 Westminster Confession and Subordinate Documents," www.apuritansmind.com/westminster-standards/shorter-catechism.

2

Only a Family can Fulfil the Church's Purpose

'This church feels like a family!' enthused Jen after church recently. It is an exceptional Sunday when we do not have new people at our church plant in Point Chevalier in Auckland, New Zealand, and this is what we regularly hear from them afterwards. This makes us very happy, because making a family out of those who come along doesn't happen by accident. We are mindful of strengthening our family bonds every time we meet.

Institutions can do a lot of stuff, but the church's core identity is not discovered in its organisational charts and strategic plans. Every church is irreducibly a family, as strong or as weak as the web of relationships that bind it together. When church behaves like a true family it can do what no other organisation can do—offer authentic belonging to hurting, distrustful people and allow them to be eyewitnesses to God's Kingdom in action.

This isn't just pie-in-the-sky. It is thoroughly biblical. If we desire to fulfil God's purpose for the church, then being family is core to our success.

A CHURCH EXPERIMENT

Four years ago, the *Love Your Neighbour* team went to churches within a reasonable radius of Point Chevalier and challenged congregations with a simple proposition. We invited folk with an adventurous, pioneering spirit who wanted to help start a church from scratch to commit to being with us for just one year. Because we would be an evening church, they wouldn't have to stop attending their morning church. When we launched, we had a core of twenty people borrowed from eight different churches and five different denominations. We met in the building of a church that had closed; the address was 126 Point Chevalier Road, so we called ourselves *church@onetwosix*. Although some individuals knew each other, we were essentially a roomful of strangers united by our desire to be a missional community in Point Chevalier.

We had recruited a bunch of activists and created urgency by setting our time frame, so understandably some wanted to jump into outreach activities straight away. What the *Love Your Neighbour* team wanted to do, however, was create a model of church that was centred in mission, not just be a church that occasionally did missional things. To do this we had to help those who were already connected to another church become a church family for the sake of Point Chevalier.

How we woo people to Jesus is by inviting them to spend time in the company of His family. Invitation is part of our culture, so we expect visitors every time we gather. We give them a name badge like everyone else and draw them in. Every Sunday evening, we begin with communion to centre us in Jesus. Over the next forty-five minutes, we eat together. It's a potluck dinner, so you never quite know what will be on the menu. The food is important to some of our guests, but for our church family the purpose of the meal is growing relationships. Over the dinner tables we take the time to get to know each other and our guests too.

As dinner is cleared away, we transition to family time and begin by welcoming our guests and giving them and those who invited them a round of applause. We use a roving microphone so that the family can share what is on their heart and tell stories of the power of God at work in our own lives and the lives of others.

We then turn to God in prayer and worship. We distribute Bibles and read the Word together at our tables. After some teaching, we include our guests in the conversation as we discuss in groups how to apply the passage in our lives today. Then we pray a benediction upon the gathering before we leave.

What I have just described probably doesn't sound much different to your church, but I don't want you to miss this. Of our two hours together on Sunday, one hour and forty minutes is devoted to family interaction. This is not just a regular service with a meal before or after. It's a family on a journey together that wants to minister into each other's lives and into the lives of the friends they bring along. They need time, guidance, and a supportive environment to be able to have the conversations that matter most.

Through the week there are other opportunities for the family to be together such as a Connect Group on Tuesdays and a 'games and crafts night' on Thursdays, but what we want to see is the family inviting others to share their homes and their lives. We tell those family members who are living in difficult circumstances and cannot host others that every act of hospitality requires a host and a guest; but they can be an others-focused guest who takes on the role of host when they help clear and wash up the dishes!

> This is not just a regular service with a meal before or after. It's a family on a journey together

Some keep coming back because authentic Christian community answers a deep longing we all have to belong. Moving from being an outsider to being an insider takes time because pride and fear stand in the way. The Holy Spirit uses the Gospel, personal circumstances, and the stories of others to confront the pride issue; but as a family we can allay fears by demonstrating love. Whoever they are and whatever their past, they are safe with us and we care about them.

Craig's story

A hip operation spelled trouble for Craig's career as a scaffolder. His two subsequent scaffolding jobs didn't work out because, as he put it, he wasn't able to 'get into top gear.' Finding himself on the street and on 'the benefit,' he started to congregate with the local homeless people. One of these was Jayson, who attended *church@onetwosix*.

Craig recalls his first encounter with the church.

> 'On the day, it was getting to be late afternoon. I was very hungry, and my friend Jayson suggested we go to the church for a meal. The first thing I noticed was that there were people of all ages there and it was very welcoming.

> 'Some of the first people I met were (a couple from) the local retirement home. They asked me about my story and almost immediately prayed for me. I was deeply touched by this and became emotional—I found myself weeping. Looking over to my friend, I asked, "Did you see that?" He was unfazed and continued eating his food. "That happens to me all the time, Craig," he replied.

> 'I was inspired by the experience. I began attending regularly and helped clear up and wash the dishes. After a quick excursion outside to have a cigarette with Jayson we would go back inside for the worship, sharing and message time in the auditorium.

> 'I found the services moving. They were relaxed and friendly and felt like family meeting together. The three guys who lead—Murray, Bruce and Howard—always shared the Gospel. I was impressed by how it was run—the openness, trust and the interest shown in me by the leaders as well as their wives and family and all the friendly people who go there, regardless of age or ethnicity. This allowed me to be myself and to freely talk, regardless of whether it was quite on point or not!

> 'Still out of work, I continued to meet more of the less-fortunate people living in the Point Chevalier area. I spent time with them and heard their stories. I feel great empathy for them. Having finally called it quits on my vocation I was keen to somehow be used by God to help these people.'

Craig was one of the first to be baptised by *church@onetwosix*. 'It was a long time coming,' says Craig. 'I had always had a sense that God was there, but I came to a time in my life when I wanted Him to direct and guide my steps and to use me to help grow His Kingdom.'

The church provided some initial avenues for Craig to serve in the community and he has gone on to find others for himself.

As Craig's story demonstrates, church as an others-focused family fulfils its missional purpose naturally. When the family knows its purpose, mission can be as simple as inviting a friend and letting the family do what it does best. Everyone in the family has a role to play, and most find it intuitively. We get to see the Gospel changing lives right in front of us where we can all see it. As people come to faith and the core of true followers of Jesus grows, our faith in the power of the Gospel grows too and we can trust God for greater things. We all rejoice together when someone is saved because we have all been on the journey with them.

CHURCH IS MEANT TO BE TRUE FAMILY

Every church, whatever its size, should be centred in family-building. Here's why:

Jesus called His disciples family

The notion that followers of Jesus are family begins with Jesus Himself.

In Mark 3, we have an account of Jesus being mobbed in a house to the extent that He and His disciples can't even eat. Jesus has started out in public ministry and His miracles and teaching are pulling in the crowds.

But Jesus' own family are not won over yet. They may not go so far as to say Jesus is possessed, as the teachers of the law do (v30), but they do fear He is crazy. His mother and brothers arrive, probably thinking to rescue Him from this intolerable situation. Not wanting to make a scene they send in someone else to call Him. 'Your mother and brothers are outside looking for you,' they say. 'Who are my mother and my brothers?' Jesus asks. Then He pointedly looks at those seated in a huddle around Him and says, 'Here are my mother and my brothers! Whoever does God's will is my brother and sister and mother' (Mark 3:31-35).

Even in a culture where family ties are much weaker than they were in Jesus' time, we feel the sting of this rebuke to His natural family who are not yet His disciples. Jesus doesn't long for home somewhere else. He is already home with His family, those who join Him in His mission of doing God's will.

At another point Jesus declares that those who convert to Christianity at great relational cost will receive many times more brothers, sisters, parents, and children in the present age (Luke 18:29–30). How is this possible? It is through the alternative family of the church that we find the substitute relationships for those that we have lost.

Jesus' closest disciples embraced this teaching, living together as an itinerant family, sharing a common purse and a common sense of identity and purpose. At the Last Supper before his crucifixion Jesus institutes a new meal-time sacrament for His disciples, the shared understanding being that these same people will continue to hang out and eat together indefinitely. They have been made into a family and will continue to do life together like a real family after He is gone.

The early church understood they were family

The Bible uses many lovely word pictures to describe the church. The imagery of the church as a body or a temple or a bride is meant metaphorically, but there is one stunning description of the church that is so commonplace it is easy to overlook, and it is not just meant figuratively. The church is a family!

This family has God as Father, Jesus as our older brother and around us are our brothers and sisters. References to 'Father' or family references such as 'brothers and sisters' or 'sons and daughters' or 'children' to address those in the church occur hundreds of times. In fact, the language of family is found in every book of the New Testament.[i]

In Acts 2 we see that the earliest Christians took the call to be family quite literally. Their first impulse was to sell off their possessions and to live as a single extended family with doors open to each other, sharing meals and working together in mission.

Being family with particular people in a particular place is meant to be 'real' — and not just in some spiritual sense. There are countless passages in

Scripture that encourage us as the church to live out the values and attributes of a good, functional family who:

- put family first (Galatians 6:10)

- take pride in each other (2 Corinthians 7:4, 2 Corinthians 9:2, 2 Thessalonians 1:4)

- have each other's back (Philippians 2:4)

- bear with each other and show forgiveness (Colossians 3:13)

- share a family table, a hospitable place (Hebrews 13:1-2)

- are mutually accountable and encourage each other (Hebrews 10:25, Matthew 18:15-17)

- offer practical support in hard times (1 John 3:17)

- mentor each other and share wisdom (Titus 2)

- deal with conflict constructively (Galatians 6:1-2).

Consider too that our natural families are temporal, but our spiritual family is eternal. Which is more 'real'? God's family is not a reflection of natural family, which many find hurtful and disappointing. Rather, natural family is meant to reflect the perfect union that already exists in the Godhead and which we as God's children will all share when we too are made perfect. We are still imperfect, yet the eternal future that we will share together has already begun for the family of God. We are in practice now for the perfection to come!

The church at its best, relating as real family, is a beautiful thing. It is not beautiful because it is perfect; it is beautiful because it is a coherent community of broken people. As Tim Chester writes, we know we are part of the family when we 'love the unlovely, forgive the unforgivable, embrace the repulsive, include the awkward, accept the weird.'[ii] For the Christian it is the place where we are understood, accepted, encouraged, supported and accountable; for those still seeking it is a peek through the window at what life in the Kingdom of God looks like. It is highly compelling for those with hearts hungry for God.

Church as family is redemptive for insiders

Being part of a church that takes family seriously has real implications for me. It helps me live out my life purpose. It helps me grow spiritually and mentor others. And mission to the world, instead of being something that I must shoulder alone (or leave to some designated church leader to do) becomes something we can all joyfully share in together.

Galatians 6:1-10 is a scripture that speaks plainly about the redemptive nature of life in the family of God:

> *Dear brothers and sisters, if another believer is overcome by some sin, you who are godly should gently and humbly help that person back onto the right path. And be careful not to fall into the same temptation yourself. Share each other's burdens, and in this way obey the law of Christ. If you think you are too important to help someone, you are only fooling yourself. You are not that important.*

> *Pay careful attention to your own work, for then you will get the satisfaction of a job well done, and you won't need to compare yourself to anyone else. For we are each responsible for our own conduct.*

> *Those who are taught the word of God should provide for their teachers, sharing all good things with them.*

> *Don't be misled—you cannot mock the justice of God. You will always harvest what you plant. Those who live only to satisfy their own sinful nature will harvest decay and death from that sinful nature. But those who live to please the Spirit will harvest everlasting life from the Spirit. So let's not get tired of doing what is good. At just the right time we will reap a harvest of blessing if we don't give up.*

> *Therefore, whenever we have the opportunity, we should do good to everyone—especially to those in the family of faith.*

As a loving family, we constantly look for ways to do each other good. From this passage we learn that when church is true family, we know the good and the bad of each other's story well enough for sinful attitudes to be confronted in love and for restoration and forgiveness to be freely sought and given. It is where helpful words of wisdom can instruct us, and where our sincere efforts and good works can be mutually encouraged. All of this knocks the rough edges off us and helps us grow spiritually. Such deep knowing of each other only comes from spending time together and being willing, out of love for the other, to sometimes press into uncomfortable territory despite the possibility of causing offence.

We belong to each other

Our experience of family shapes how we think of it. It is an emotional and relational word that reaches beyond simply being 'blood relatives.' There are so many examples of those who serve as caring family for others, but one way that unrelated people become family is through adoption. This is how we join the family of God (Ephesians 1:5).

In a functional family, everyone plays a role and contributes, both practically and socially. Likewise, the role that each church family member plays shapes the dynamic of that family. Our presence and our absence, therefore, make a real difference.

In 1 Corinthians 12, Paul uses the metaphor of the body to describe this. Some of us are 'eyes,' others are 'feet,' or 'noses'—we each have a unique purpose. In Romans 12, he points out that we, the various body parts, form one body in which we all belong to each other; and we are each given different gifts according to God's grace which we are to exercise for the benefit of the whole family (v5-8). Our church family, therefore, uniquely provides the space where we can usefully minister to others—and be meaningfully ministered to ourselves.

> Intimate bonds within the family can only be forged if I can depend on you and you can depend on me

Belonging *to* each other runs counter to our cultural thinking. How can it be that I have a claim on you and you on me? In his mind, church is clearly more than a voluntary association like a gym or tennis club. The kind of belonging Paul speaks of more closely resembles marriage and family—it is an everyday commitment.

Intimate bonds within the family can only be forged if I can depend on you and you can depend on me, where I have covenanted to be there for you, and you for me. If I can't count on my 'Jesus family,' why should I invest there? Why should I open up and share honestly and deeply?

It is part of our Christian discipleship that we be fully committed to building the church as Jesus envisioned it—a place where I am accountable to others and they are accountable to me; where I am responsible to others and they are responsible to me; where I count on them and they count on me. As it turns out, I am my brother's keeper.

Philip Yancey says, 'It is in the family of God that I am able to care and be cared for; love and be loved; forgive and be forgiven; rebuke and be rebuked; encourage and be encouraged—all of which is essential to the task of being a disciple of the risen Lord Jesus.'[iii]

We are meant to work together

In an individualistic culture, we can easily read verses that were written to whole churches and take only a personal application from them. In Philippians 2:12-16 for example, Paul had the whole church family in mind. Note that 'you' and 'your' are all plural:

> *Dear friends, you always followed my instructions when I was with you. And now that I am away, it is even more important. Work hard to show the results of your salvation, obeying God with deep reverence and fear. For God is working in you, giving you the desire and the power to do what pleases him. Do everything without complaining and arguing, so that no one can criticize you.*

Live clean, innocent lives as children of God, shining like bright lights in a world full of crooked and perverse people. Hold firmly to the word of life; then, on the day of Christ's return, I will be proud that I did not run the race in vain and that my work was not useless.

Paul is enjoining the church to be on this journey together as family. In so doing, he encourages us, we will fulfil God's purposes and be a light to our world.

Ephesians 4:1-16 also illustrates how, as we work on being Christ's family in the power and strength of the Spirit, we are equipped together for works of service which in turn help all of us grow and mature. When we are together, doing the good works for which we were created and which God planned beforehand for us to do (Ephesians 2:10), we are fulfilling our purpose.

Church as a family is redemptive for outsiders

God's mission through His church begins and ends with family. A family reaches out and draws others in so that they become family too. What we desire for our friends is that they come and join us. The whole family shares this anticipation.

This what the apostle John is getting at in 1 John 1:3-4 *(emphasis mine):*

*We proclaim to you what we ourselves have actually seen and heard so that you may have fellowship with us. And our fellowship is with the Father and with his Son, Jesus Christ. We are writing these things so that you **may fully share our joy.***

The church's mission is not just outside the walls where it gathers. The family gathered is itself a powerful witness to a watching world. Matthew 5:14-16 is another passage that hints at our witness as a community, not just as individuals. Once again, the words 'you' and 'your' are plural:

You are the light of the world—like a city on a hilltop that cannot be hidden. No one lights a lamp and then puts it under a basket. Instead, a lamp is placed on a stand, where it gives light to everyone in the house. In the same way, let your good deeds shine out for all to see, so that everyone will praise your heavenly Father (Matthew 5:14-16).

Here Jesus looks at future members of His church and tells them that the things they will do together will be seen by others as evidence of God at work. The 'city on a hill' imagery of a myriad twinkling lights gathered in one place shining out into a darkness is a beautiful picture of how we together as family are the light of the world.

Jesus also said that the watching world would know that we are His disciples because they observe two marvellous characteristics; they will marvel at our love for each other (John 13:35), and they will marvel at our unity (John 17:23). He anticipated that onlookers would see the gathered church being real family and be drawn to it.

There is no finer example of the saving power of a real church family than the passage we looked at in the last chapter. Let me quote it again for easy reference:

> *All the believers devoted themselves to the apostles' teaching, and to fellowship, and to sharing in meals (including the Lord's Supper), and to prayer. A deep sense of awe came over them all, and the apostles performed many miraculous signs and wonders.*
>
> *And all the believers met together in one place and shared everything they had. They sold their property and possessions and shared the money with those in need. They worshipped together at the Temple each day, met in homes for the Lord's Supper, and shared their meals with great joy and generosity—all the while praising God and enjoying the goodwill of all the people. And each day the Lord added to their fellowship those who were being saved (Acts 2:42–47).*

How do you think those who are 'being saved' in this passage are coming to salvation? Are they being saved 'on camera,' inside the frame of what Luke is describing—or are they being saved 'off camera,' in another place, at another time? If the latter is true, it is strange that Luke the historian would give us such a detailed account of what the church did when they were together, yet be mysteriously silent about the important work of evangelism happening in the wings that served as their engine for growth.

I believe Luke is telling us everything we need to know. Notice the cycle between two locales—the public spaces (temple and marketplace) where ordinary people gathered; and their homes, where they gathered as church family. The implication of this passage is that, through invitation and hospitality, outsiders met a family on fire for God. Brought to the fire, they themselves caught alight! Spontaneous evangelism by individuals in their personal world undoubtedly occurred, but it appears that experiencing God's gathered family overflowing with the Holy Spirit was the regular way people were saved.

> As it was for the first century church, the answer still lies in invitation and hospitality

Our church family may be a powerful witness, but how will outsiders know unless they get a chance to experience us? As it was for the first century church, the answer still lies in invitation and hospitality.

The family keeps empty seats at the family table that they are longing to fill. As guests are invited and experience a loving family, the Holy Spirit continues His work in them. Wooed to Jesus, many will return again and again until by God's grace they too become family.

In the West, we tend to imagine ourselves as lone rangers in our individual worlds, each contending for the Gospel, with church as a kind of refuelling station. However, mission described in the New Testament is usually undertaken by a cadre of friends; the exceptions are always due to special circumstances (such as Paul being in prison, or Philip being carried into the desert).

Our encounters with the people whom God sends across our path may begin with just us, but we need to know that our church family also cares about, and wants to share, these relationships.

Mission is how those we befriend in our world become part of the family of God. God is already at work in the lives of the people we meet; our part of the process starts with personal befriending. Then, through invitation and hospitality (and the application of Godly wisdom) we introduce them to our

Christian family friends, trusting that by God's grace we will woo them to our church family table.

This approach to mission isn't only more doable, it is sensible. Relationships can be hard work. All of us have a limited capacity to add new relationships to our lives, especially if those people are 'high need.' However, if we can share our relationships with others in our church family, then we can sustainably befriend many more people between us.

This has the double benefit of immediately introducing our seeking friends to a wider network of Christians, thereby multiplying the number of 'God conversations' they will have and making it far more likely that they will leave their existing safety net and make the leap of faith into ours.

But there is also a bigger question. When I lead someone to Christ, what comes next? It is lifelong discipleship, and this is a process I cannot do alone. I need my church family to be warm and welcoming so that my new disciple can be introduced to the rest of my support network and enjoy the life-changing reality of being part of the family themselves.

The aim, therefore, of the Gospel is to bring people into relationship with Jesus and His church. Experiencing the reality of a community which passionately loves God, each other, and the not-yet-saved, can win over the hearts of the lost before their heads have even fully comprehended the message of salvation. As they journey with us, their understanding will grow; the truth is, the good news continues to get bigger and bigger for every Christian as we grow in the grace and knowledge of Jesus.

Let's remember that it was God's plan to put us in church families where everyone can play their part and exercise the special, miraculous gifts God has given them—not only for the benefit of those already within the faith, but also for the redemption of those on the outside looking in.

OUR WORLD DESPERATELY NEEDS A FAMILY

'Belongingness' is a real word! It describes everyone's deep emotional need to be an important part of something greater than themselves. It is the need to give and receive attention. Mere acquaintance or familiarity won't do.

Abraham Maslow considered 'belonging' to be one of five basic human needs. According to Maslow, our most basic needs relate to our survival; these are our physiological and safety needs. But the next most important need of any individual is the need to belong and be loved. This need must be met before one can properly address our need for self-esteem and self-actualisation.[iv]

Further research has found that there are two main features to belongingness. First, people need constant, positive, personal interactions with other people. Second, people need to know that the bond is stable, there is mutual concern, and that this attachment will continue. Individuals need to know that other people truly care about their well-being and love them.[v]

What we are experiencing in New Zealand society has been described as 'an epidemic of loneliness'—in fact, the number of close friends the average person relates to has halved in the last twenty years.[vi] The reality is that while we crave deep connection with other human beings with whom we can share our story, we live in a self-focused, attention-deficient world.

It turns out that friends who are orbiting at the farthest reaches of our digital galaxy cannot solve our real-world loneliness. The vital friendships—the people we hug and laugh and lament with and who know the unvarnished truth about us—are the ones who have the greatest impact on our health and happiness. The lonely people in our world need a family where they can belong, have a purpose, and contribute their unique gifting. Who other than the church family is willing to offer this kind of radical, messy, time-consuming hospitality? Taking the time to hear the story of our neighbours,

> It is not our accommodation to our culture that makes us relevant. It is our unconditional love for those we invite to the family table

and relating their story to the story of Jesus is perhaps the greatest missional opportunity of our age.

Churches often fret about their relevance to the culture or how much they have to offer. But it is not our accommodation to our culture that makes us relevant. It is our unconditional love for those we invite to the family table and our constancy in living out the values of the Kingdom together that make us 'a city on a hill.'

BEING TRUE FAMILY FULFILS THE CHURCH'S PURPOSE

I believe that when the church is building up insiders and wooing outsiders with the Gospel of Jesus, God is being glorified. Any church for which this is true is fulfilling its purpose. The model given in Scripture that helps us achieve these related goals with the greatest success and with the least impediment, is church as family. These twin goals are brought together beautifully and simply by the concept of a family table, a place where people eagerly and deliberately gather to eat and share the stories of their day. If a church is to experience being family together, chances are, it will look just like that!

Some churches eat meals together, but if your church does not or cannot do this, then some other regular, customary way of experiencing family is needed. We are talking about an unhurried

Everyone who comes should experience family, not just a church service

space integral to your time together where conversations about the things that matter most can happen. This requires thought, intentionality and creativity. The guiding principle is that everyone who comes should experience family, not just a church service.

Whatever your 'family table' practice becomes, it is then a small step to invite outsiders to come and experience your church family in a way that lets them see the spiritual reality on the inside, rather than just the form and ritual on the outside. In this way our table serves both a family and a missional purpose.

Let's recap what I have outlined through this chapter:

- God's mission mandate is given to a collective—His church—for a reason. It is too big for any of us to do alone. Together we can share the load, each play our part, be mutually encouraged, see our faith grow, and build a movement.

- The church as family is alluded to in every book of the New Testament, and it's not just a metaphor. God's mission is given to 'us' not just 'me.' It is meant to be done together as a family.

- Before we can reach out to save others, we need a secure foundation. The family gives us a durable place to belong and have a ministry to others. It is a safe place where we are known and accountable.

- The heart of the family is the family table where we spend unhurried time together, each sometimes playing the role of host and sometimes as guest. My story becomes part of the story of my family. The family is a different shape for accommodating me and would miss me if I was not there.

- The family also equips each other for mission. It is a place where good behaviours and practices are modelled and learned. It is a hospitable place that eagerly invites others, and is a powerful witness to those who experience it.

- Mission is the process by which outsiders come in to become family with us. This is also the heart need of the people in our world—to belong in a family.

NINE WAYS WE CAN MAKE OUR CHURCH MORE LIKE FAMILY

1. Use the language of family

Our words make our worlds. By using the language of family, the culture and identity of your church will begin to grow in this direction. Be relentless! At the point you become tired of using them, your words will just be beginning to sink in.

2. Make church family-sized

I am told the average New Zealand church has fewer than seventy adherents. If your church is average by this metric, then rejoice! You are a great size with huge potential as a church family on a mission together. Don't try and replicate the model of 'big church'—if you don't have the people-resources to make it work, you will just burn people out. Your strength lies in relationship and being a family.

If God's plan for His church is that we be a family on a mission together, then we need to make it work, whatever our church size. Bigger churches may have to work harder at creating family-sized units within the larger whole in order to provide a place for everyone to belong and share life and mission as family. We grow by multiplying family-sized units, either as new church plants or by creating new units.

3. Integrate family time in your service

If we simply tack 'family time' onto the beginning or the end of our regular service, we make it optional. Many will choose to skip this bit, believing that only the 'traditional church' part is essential. To change the culture of our church, we need to make participation in family life inescapable. It may feel strange at first, but soon everyone will come to love it (except perhaps for Uncle Todd, but then, there's no pleasing him!). You will become the kind of church that no-one wants to leave.

4. Hold family councils, not business meetings

As we will explore later, the members of a church are not there to support the mission of the church, as much as the other way around—the church family mutually supports the mission of its members. It is therefore vital that we find safe, inclusive ways of getting everyone to contribute to the big decisions surrounding the family's direction and practice. General business meetings cannot always be avoided, but they are the least safe and least inclusive way of making decisions. Far better to approximate a family council meeting around the dining table, than a business meeting with an agenda, a microphone, and rules of order.

5. Be a place that people can bring their friends home to

Remember bringing your friends home from school? Church should also be a place where our friends are expected and welcomed. As in a regular family, we need to talk together about how we will behave when we have guests with us. We need to be others-focused by including them in our circle and being appropriately curious and interested in them. Our stance towards guests should be that of wooers—we have the privilege of becoming part of their faith journey, we never take offence, and we never get defensive. We demonstrate that the church 'home' is a safe and nurturing place.

6. Model good behaviour, call out bad behaviour

Church is a meeting of family rather than an event because its purpose is relational: to grow disciples and woo friends to Jesus. We help grow each other to maturity in Christ and gain competency by being the kind of 'parent' that Paul was (1 Thessalonians 2:6-12). We model good behaviour to one another, and we publicly praise each other. We are also willing to risk offense by talking to offenders privately about their bad behaviour—we do so for the sake of their own spiritual growth and to preserve the integrity and witness of the family. We don't expect guests to behave like Christians, but we have a higher standard for family.

7. As far as you are able, give everyone a job to do

The active family model of church is the polar opposite of the passive consumer model. The goal of church is not to run like a well-oiled machine, but to be engaging and valuing of people and relationships. Be willing to sacrifice efficiency and lower your standards in order to give everyone a job. Everyone wants to make a contribution and be needed.

8. Be flexible and opportunistic

Church is where we respond to need and opportunity as most families do. Rally around when someone in the family needs help, and support those who are trying to reach out to others. Keep your ear to the ground in your community and do what you can.

As people come and go and the family keeps changing, so should our plans. Family-sized churches can have long-term intentions but should not make long-term plans. We need to constantly adapt our plans to a changing environment. Life is fluid and people are transient.

9. Have fun

While we are serious about fulfilling our God-given purpose, we don't take ourselves too seriously. Our best family memories are of the times we got silly and laughed till we cried. We must never be frivolous about the important things, but it is important that we sometimes have fun!

---

[i] Matthew 5:9, Mark 3:3, Luke 6:35, John 1:12, Acts 1:16, Romans 9:26, 1 Corinthians 1:1, 2 Corinthians 1:1, Galatians 3:26, Ephesians 3:6, Philippians 1:2, Colossians 1:1-2, 1 Thessalonians 1:3-4, 2 Thessalonians 1:2-3, 1 Timothy 1:2, 2 Timothy 1:2, Titus 1:4, Philemon 1-3, Hebrews 12:7, James 2:15, 1 Peter 1:22, 2 Peter 1:10, 1 John 4:7, 2 John. 3, 3 John 3, Revelation 12:10
[ii] Tim Chester, *Total Church* (SPCK, 2012), 111.
[iii] Quoted in Tim Chester, *Total Church* (SPCK, 2012).
[iv] 'Maslow's Hierarchy of Needs,' *Wikipedia*, May 4, 2020, accessed May 5, 2020.
[v] Roy F Baumeister and Mark R Leary, 'The Need to Belong,' *Psychological Bulletin* 117, no. 3 (1995).
[vi] Taken from an article by Catherine Woulfe, 'The perils of ignoring the spiral of loneliness,' *Noted*, July 24, 2016, www.noted.co.nz/currently/currently-social-issues/the-perils-of-ignoring-the-spiral-of-loneliness

3

Embracing our Place

I n this book I describe a particular vision of church—church as a *family* in a *place* on a *mission together*. We have looked at what it means to be a family, but in order to explore the church's everyday mission, we need to first examine what it means to be grounded in a place.

Perhaps the New Zealand church's problem is its lack of groundedness. We are hazy about our mission and purpose, we undervalue God's gift of church family, and we are often unaware of the ground we are worshipping upon—the geographic and social 'soil' in which God has planted our particular church family. Without these tangibles there is little to anchor us and people drift away.

So what do we need to do if we are going to re-ground our practice of church?

We need to embrace our purpose

We began this book by considering that our core purpose as Christians (and hence as Christ's church) is to glorify God in the world. 'Glorify' and 'worship' are often treated as synonyms, but while they are closely related, the roots of these words point to their difference. The first comes from the Latin *gloria* which means fame or renown; the second is from an old English word *weordscipe* which means 'to revere or venerate.' Yes, venerating and adoring Jesus is part of our God-glorifying mission, but it is not our whole mission. Our larger purpose is to glorify God by doing the works He gave us to do and by witnessing to His presence in the world, not just worshipping Him in the house. A church that embraces this larger purpose will also be a worshipping community. However, it is only too easy to be a worshipping community that loses sight of mission.

Placing mission at the heart of church means prioritising time for relationship-building, because our mission is all about connecting with people. We can't simply put a mission statement on the wall and lapse into familiar, time-worn practices that leave no time to talk. We need to restructure our time in a way that acknowledges that we are on a people-gathering mission together.

We need to embrace our problem

Much of our current practice in the Western church is based on an individualistic understanding of salvation and mission, in which our lives are to be lived 'you in your small corner and I in mine.'

With an individualistic starting point, the purpose of the Sunday gathering can be understood to be primarily about me: a time to have *my* flagging spirits restored through songs of praise and worship and to have *my* tank refilled through Bible teaching so that I can go back to *my* world revived. When we view church through this lens, we come to church as consumers seeking to have our own needs met.

What we prioritise in church may be signalling that this understanding of 'consumer church' is correct and all that is required of the 'faithful' is 'faithful attendance.' A church consciously or unconsciously operating on this premise puts its effort into those elements of the service that its people are coming to consume, such as the worship music and the preaching. Under this model, however, the only people who are truly needed are those who are helping produce what will be consumed.

This reality feeds the modern trend of only attending church occasionally. If we go to church to receive rather than because we are needed there, we will consider skipping church if we are not feeling spiritually needy—or conversely, not feeling spiritual enough. The decision whether to attend church is being made fifty-two times a year; it is no longer habitual as it once was when for many church people, faithful attendance was considered a sacred duty.

Church for consumers can also be anywhere, needing only a suitable venue that brings together church people and the resources needed to provide the spiritual services on offer. The question of where this church is located is driven by economics and ease of access, rather than a desire to be grounded in a place.

If our current model of church was working, the Christian church in New Zealand would not be in decline. What will restore its vitality? A big step in the right direction would be to trade transactional relationships (where people come for the spiritual services we provide) for the truly functional relationships of family, where everyone is needed and plays a part.

We need to embrace our church as family

We saw in the last chapter that the Christian's purpose of glorifying God is not ours to live out alone. Two precious gifts are helpful and necessary if we are to successfully fulfil our purpose. The first is the gift of the Holy Spirit, the seal of our salvation, who indwells us. God Himself empowers us and leads us into all truth. The other gift is that of a church family, the real flesh and blood people we need for mutual discipleship and encouragement in the faith. We complement each other as we live out our purpose together.

> Understanding that the church's mission was given to a family has implications for how we do church

Understanding that the church's mission was given to a family has implications for how we do church. We don't come to church to worship with the lights off so that we can get into a personal, private 'zone' with God. Our personal piety should be something we work on every day, not just on Sundays. We come together to commune with God *and* others. This requires that we interact and look into each other's eyes. We must both give and receive from each other and use our spiritual gifts to deal with the grounded realities of being this family in this place right now.

We need to embrace our place

This raises another important matter, and here we begin breaking new ground. If we are really meant to be a family on a mission, where is this family when it is home? Where does our church family belong? And does God have a purpose for us being *here*, rather than somewhere else?

This is a question seldom asked by Western churches. They know where they meet and they may be doing outreach in a particular area, but does the church belong there?

If we understand church to be the space where individual Christians congregate for the sake of their personal piety and the institutional mission of the church, then all we need is a building in a convenient location; questions of belonging to a place as a church are nonsensical.

However, if our church family wishes to be centred in glorifying mission, we need to take place seriously. All mission is to *particular people* in a *particular place*. Unless our church family takes belonging to a place seriously, we drastically hinder our ability to fulfil God's purpose in planting us there. So let's investigate this blind spot.

WHAT DO WE MEAN BY 'PLACE'?

In many indigenous people groups around the world there is a special appreciation of place and its power to bind society through a sense of belonging. They prize a harmonious relationship between the land (which they respect) and the people who live there. Having lived long on the land, 'place' for them is imbued with history and meaning. Dwelling richly in the land, and not just on it, is for them an essential aspect of human wellbeing.

Western society once valued place too, but the personal freedom granted to us by fast and efficient transport that allows us to inhabit spaces in many different places (we can be half a world away within the same day!) has dulled our sense of place. Rapid transit and 24/7 digital connection seem to have shrunk the globe, the forces of globalisation duping us into thinking that the whole world is one global village with everyone equally sharing in a global economy.

Modern Western thinking ties human wellbeing to endless economic growth, an idea the church seems willing to bless despite the detriment to our earth and to poorer societies who pay the price for our consumerism. From within this framework land is no more than a commodity to be used and sold at will.

The church needs to rediscover God's purposes for our places of belonging and its role in human flourishing.

Place is more than a location, and the land that undergirds place is so much more than dirt. Land is part of God's good creation, helping to sustain all life on the planet, including ours. When we fail to see past the concrete and asphalt to God's good gift of the land, we become thoughtless towards the land and thankless towards God for it.

Place and belonging

The relationship between the land and the people who dwell there gives every place a unique history and character. We shape our places and they, in turn, shape us. Our experience of life, as well as our imagination of what the good life looks like, is tied to place. For example, whether we live at the coast or in an inland mining town fundamentally alters the kind of society we will find there.

Moving to New Zealand twenty-five years ago, my family was delighted with the country. The lush green landscape and regular rain perfectly fitted our ideal of the good life. However, a fellow countrywoman of our acquaintance who moved at a similar time simply could not settle. She came from the Karoo, an arid part of South Africa where the landscape is dotted with thorn trees and the colour palette is shades of brown and grey-green.

'The green is driving me crazy!' she would exclaim, experiencing psychic pain from the very landscape we were finding intoxicatingly beautiful. She eventually felt she had to return to the place and the people whose dreams and values she shared.

Of course, every place is continually evolving and changing, but those who live there experience continuity because they are part of the story. To know a place is to understand why things are the way they are, which only comes from spending time there. In the process we are both shaped by the place and leave our own imprint on it so that in some small way the place is different because of us. That is what it means to belong.

Belonging and place go together. One of the first questions we ask of someone new is, 'where are you from?' We ask the question because knowing where they belong tells us something important about them. Their story and history have been shaped by the place they come from. A stranger is someone out of place, someone who has come from a place where they did belong but is now rootless in a place they don't belong.

Rootedness in place and community is God's design

The Old Testament tells the overarching story of how God rescued His homeless people, Israel, and gave them a land and a home. When God later instructs them to care for strangers and aliens, it is a reminder that Israel was once exactly that themselves. God doesn't want us to live rootless lives. Rootedness in place and community is God's design.

When we are blind to place, the church can be guilty of being 'colonial,' trying to minister from our framework of understanding in places where we do not yet belong and without seeking to understand the story of the place or connecting with the faithful ones who have been ministering God's grace to this place long before us.

In the early days of *church@onetwosix*, we as leaders were keen on the idea of running a 'vegetable co-op,' sourcing pre-ordered quantities of fruit and vegetables directly from growers for the benefit of the community, as a means of building relationships with the folk of Point Chevalier. It was an idea that was successfully bringing church and community together elsewhere in the country.

When someone from a grower's market approached us, wanting to bring this exact service to our suburb, we were certain God was in it. It was only when we experienced a total lack of enthusiasm from the locals that we learned that there had been a vegetable co-op in Point Chevalier for many years which had run its course and finally shut down, with those who had been running it feeling thoroughly worn out. Without this knowledge of our place's history, we were on the brink of wasting a great deal of time, energy, and money.

For its own sake and for the sake of the Gospel, we need to re-inhabit places as local churches, becoming immersed in the story of the place we belong in. Let's look at why this is true.

GOD, PEOPLE, PLACE

God's salvation story with humankind has always been played out within the angles of this triangle:

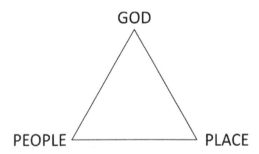

In the beginning, God created Adam and Eve and placed them in the Garden of Eden. He gave them a purpose in being there—the role of stewardship for that place. There they enjoyed pure communion with God as He walked in the garden with them.

Later there was another beginning, as God promised that He would raise from Abraham a great family-nation and give the land on which Abraham was standing to them as a place to call their own. They would be His people and He would be their God.

From Sinai, God gave His people laws that demonstrate how these three aspects are intertwined for God's covenant people. A violation against society or against the land that God has given is also a violation of the covenant with God and must be dealt with by God's covenant people. In Deuteronomy 22:5-7, a prohibition against cross-dressing (social behaviour) is immediately followed by a prohibition against taking a mother bird from sitting on her eggs or chicks (care of place), yet there is no incongruity, because the wellbeing of God's people and the sustainability of the land which God gave them as a gift are tied together under His lordship in a glorifying whole . . . *God, People, Place.*

Let's jump to the end of the story for a moment. One day when Christ returns and all things have been renewed, every place will fall within this triangle. All people will proclaim Christ as Lord and will be in right relationship with each other and with all of creation. With the effects and shackles of sin finally done away with, the new heaven and new earth will be joined together in perfect balance and harmony.

> The wellbeing of God's people and the sustainability of the land which God gave them as a gift are tied together

How does all this inform what the church should be doing today? What we learn from Scripture is that God's covenantal relationship with Israel was a kind of prototype for how God would ultimately bring every nation back to Himself. There is a line of broadening revelation from Adam to Israel to the Messiah who would come as Saviour and establish a universal Kingdom of all who receive Him by faith, irrespective of race or land borders.

The church, God's 'called out' people, are tasked with extending the legacy of faithful Israel to the whole world. All who live by faith in Christ are now the covenant people of God. The church proclaims God's Kingdom and is itself a foretaste of the Kingdom to come. Every local community of believers searches the Scriptures and listens to the prompting of the Holy Spirit to discern what is pleasing to God as we live out our faith in the world.

Our efforts may be imperfect, but the church's present practice should be consonant with what has been revealed of God's will both in the past and for the future. The triangle of relationship between *God, People and Place* was true for Israel and will be true when Jesus returns in glory. If this reflects the heart of our unchanging God, it is reasonable to conclude that this triangle is not only a picture of reconciliation for the church, but also reflects His mission to the whole wide world.

The church may be universal, but it comprises local church families— particular people in particular places, under God. Similarly, the outworking of our mission is always grounded with particular people in a particular place. Missionaries like Paul started many new churches, but he left behind local church families that identified with the place where they were planted.

If we think of local church families as small '*God-People-Place*' triangles on a map, God's Kingdom grows as these triangles multiply through missionary planting until the map is covered. Our small triangles will eventually merge into one universal triangle when Jesus returns. This is what I think of when I hear Jesus saying that the Kingdom is like yeast working its way through a ball of dough until it is completely changed (Matthew 13:33).

> Missionaries like Paul started local church families that identified with the place where they were planted

Our place and our mission are intrinsically connected. Chris Wright, author and leading thinker on the mission of God, concludes that the church serves God's mission by *building the church* through evangelism and discipleship, by *serving society* as we seek compassion and justice and by *caring for creation* through Godly use of the resources of creation along with ecological concern and action.[i]

These three missional emphases make perfect sense of the interrelationship between *God, People and Place*—the three angles of the triangle I have described.

1. In *building the church*, we, the people of God, seek to proclaim the Gospel to those who co-inhabit our space and woo them to Jesus.

2. In *serving society,* we, the people of God, seek to embody, proclaim and contend for God's compassion and justice in the place where God has planted us.

3. In *caring for creation,* we, the people of God, seek to embody, proclaim and contend for good stewardship of the land which God has gifted to us and which supports and sustains all who live in our place.

All three of these emphases (spiritual, social, and our physical world) are important for human flourishing and are interlinked. Clean air and water, biodiversity and green spaces, are as vital to our wellbeing and ability to thrive as a kind and just society. In fact, social problems such as crime and depression tend to be exacerbated when we lose connection to the natural world.

Without dealing with our sin problem, however, our efforts to build a better world always fall apart. Without the church, the world misses the crucial third corner of the triangle—the healing and wholeness to be found as all things are brought under the lordship of Christ. Only the church can be the torchbearer for a holistic vision of human flourishing that includes God, people, and place.

God cares about our places

Places have significance for God, but it is not just state boundaries God cares about. It is evident from Scripture that He also cares about our more intimate places of belonging—our communities, towns, and cities. Three poignant passages spring to mind. In Jonah 4:11 God tells how deeply He cares for

> God loves your place so much that He planted your church there as part of His redemptive plan

Nineveh. Then, in Jeremiah 29:7, God's people in exile are enjoined to seek the peace and prosperity of Babylon. And in Luke 19:41-44, Jesus is moved to tears by the predicament the people of Jerusalem are in.

God recognises places as entities with their own character and values, not just as a collection of individuals. God loves your place so much that He planted your church there as part of His redemptive plan. It is no accident that your church family finds itself planted where it is. And if your church family isn't going to be a conduit of God's blessing to its neighbours, then who is?

Chances are your church was planted in a place where there was a felt need for a church. The founders no doubt thought, 'This place needs a church like ours.' If we have lost this vision of being a blessing and have metaphorically allowed weeds to grow in the place where God planted us, let us once again receive our place as a gift from the hand of God Himself and determine again to be good neighbours.

The ordinary places we know

Contentment and blessing are to be found in committing to an ordinary, imperfect place, calling it home, and seeking its welfare. They may not forever remain in one place, but wherever they go, place-builders commit to the place where they are and try to leave things a little better than they found them.

This is not only good for us socially and emotionally, but spiritually too. The best environment for our personal spiritual formation is right here—in the ordinary, imperfect place where we are, with those we didn't choose but who share this place with us.

Discontent is very human. Because of the ease with which we can now travel great distances, we fall prey to escapist thinking that something better or more suitable may be found in some other place. Instead of dreaming about the ordinary, imperfect places we know, we dream and hope for the extraordinary elsewhere. And yet, when I fly to a new overseas destination, I am struck by the fact that, after hours of plane travel, the destination I have reached also has weeds and litter and decay and rust, and the locals find it as ordinary as I do my own place back home.

Jeremy Linneman asks, 'What has mobility cost us but stability? We've lost our sense of pride in the ordinary things of life.'[ii]

He also quotes Craig Batholomew as saying, 'In our late-modern age . . . place has become something that one moves through, preferably at great speed, and virtual reality is no re-place-ment.'[iii]

Imagine your place as a field of wildflowers. In this field, we see flowers of every hue, and because it is wild, there are a good number of weeds too. When we commit to place, we embrace the whole field as God's gift to us, including the poor, the marginalised and the ungrateful. It is here that God would have us minister and be ministered to—because having to work out our spiritual walk with people who are 'other' to us confronts our unexamined assumptions, our prejudices and our selfishness. We learn to love like Christ.

G.K. Chesterton observes: 'The man who lives in a small community lives in a much larger world . . . the reason is obvious. In a large community we can choose our companions. In a small community our companions are chosen for us.'[iv]

In a world where our mobility makes it possible for us to always associate with people with whom we feel a natural affinity instead of embracing the

> A church family based on proximity is a sharper tool for discipleship than a church family based on affinity

wild field, we can choose to surround ourselves with other flowers like ourselves and be content to minister only to them. Ultimately, however, we will be the poorer for it. A church family based on proximity is a sharper tool for discipleship than a church family based on affinity. Being faithfully present in our place means to act on the belief that God is giving us what we need to be formed as disciples right where we are.

As Philip Yancey states: 'We often surround ourselves with the people we most want to live with, thus forming a club or clique, not a community. Anyone can form a club; it takes grace, shared vision and hard work to form a community.'[v]

Returning to the *God-People-Place* triangle, we can only know ourselves rightly when we first know our God. And we only know Him rightly when we know Him as sovereign Lord of all creation, who gives us our place as a gift. When we are blind to the very place God planted us and are always looking to serve elsewhere, we severely hamper our ability to partner with God, who desires mission to the people in the place where we are already.

Seeking the welfare of our place

Jeremiah 29:4-14 is an interesting passage. God's chosen people find themselves as exiles and aliens in Babylon, a place and culture used as a metaphor by the prophets to describe the antithesis of what life under God looks like. It is surprising, then, that the message God asks Jeremiah to convey to the exiles is this:

> *Build homes, and plan to stay. Plant gardens and eat the food they produce. Marry and have children. Then find spouses for them so that you may have many grandchildren. Multiply! Do not dwindle away! And work for the peace and prosperity of the city where I sent you into exile. Pray to the Lord for it, for its welfare will determine your welfare (Jeremiah 29:4-7).*

We too find ourselves as foreigners and exiles in the world (1 Peter 2:11-12) and feel the same tensions they did. Do we withdraw from the world to preserve our holiness, or do we assimilate with that world and risk losing our special identity?

The false prophets in the Jeremiah passage were saying what God's people in exile wanted to hear. They wanted out of there. Settling down, building, planting and marrying went against this dream. They imagined that by keeping themselves separate and 'pure,' God would be pleased with them and would be obligated to bring about the quick rescue they wanted.

God's perspective, however, was broader. He promised to bring back His people in His own good time—but only after they had been a blessing to the Babylonian society in which they lived. What was good for the Babylonians was also good for God's people! When we are good, productive, influential citizens who invest to make our place better, everybody wins.

This is not just a call to be a good influence or a call to good deeds alone. We are to 'pray to the Lord for the city.' We are seeking spiritual change as well as physical change. Our desire is to be fully transformational.

However, we must not lose our identity, our religious practices, or our hope of future rescue. God's message to those in exile was not that they should simply assimilate with the people around them. He wanted them remain true to their God whilst seeking the prosperity of their city of exile. For the sake of the culture, they had to live counter-culturally. We are to be 'in the world, but not of the world' (John 17:14-15). We can only make a difference by being different.

> When we are good, productive, influential citizens who invest to make our place better, everybody wins

And we must persevere. Only after seventy years had been completed in Babylon would the Lord bring the exiles back to the Promised Land. Seventy years was regarded as the entire natural lifespan of a person (Psalm 90:10) — it was a lifetime given 'for Babylon.' We must patiently invest in the place where God has planted us, even if it is not our final home.

This patient investment brings God's *shalom* to our place. *Shalom* is a Hebrew word meaning peace, harmony, wholeness, completeness, prosperity, welfare and tranquillity. Says Nicholas Wolterstorff, '*Shalom* is harmony and delight in all one's relationships — with God, with other human beings, with culture, with nature, with oneself.'[vi]

The consequences of sin have disrupted the relationships in our place and robbed it of *shalom*. Our unbelieving neighbours are out of relationship with God; there is self-centredness and self-interest at the heart of every local dispute and in every systemic injustice. Once our own hearts are right with God, God gives us the ministry of reconciliation to share with others (2 Corinthians 5). The ministry of reconciliation is the tearing down of walls so that those who were once living in enmity can live together in peace (Ephesians 2:14-16).

A vital part of our ministry of reconciliation is the clear proclamation of the message of salvation found in Jesus. Jesus said, 'What good is it if one gains the whole world but loses one's soul?' (Mark 8:36). We call to everyone in our place, including those within the family who are straying, 'Be reconciled to God!' (2 Corinthians 5:20). The only change that will last is centred in Him.

We also strive to reconcile people with each other. Where there is poverty, injustice, oppression or lack of mercy, a wall has been erected that separates people from right relationship. Jesus cares so deeply about these issues that He includes them in His own ministry manifesto—so we should too (see Luke 4:16-20).

Every time we intervene as instruments of the love of God, we bear witness to the King who reigns over our place. By turning the eyes of our neighbours who have not noticed Him before towards Him, His *invisible reign* becomes *visible realm* within our place.[vii]

RECLAIMING THE BEST OF 'PARISH'

I don't come from a church tradition that has parishes, so I may be more open to the rich possibilities of the term than someone for whom it has negative connotations.

A 'parish' is generally understood to be the bounded area served or cared for by the local church. There have been times when the concept has been used as a means of coercion, establishing boundaries for purposes of extracting payment from people or as a means of 'protecting turf'—keeping people out or in.

However, if we may reclaim the best of 'parish,' there is much in the concept to inform the practice of church in a place.

'Parish' can be a redemptive idea

- It assumes a local church embracing its place and seeking the welfare of that place.

- It is a church family living out its faith together in the same community, creating a web of relationships that tie church and community together.

- It is church putting down deep roots and choosing to be present and constant. When we are present and constant, we get to know and be known deeply. As our neighbours get to know and trust us, we become part of their story, and they part of ours.

- It is church keeping open 'God space' within the wider community where everyone is welcome and can freely belong. There is no spiritual test to enter this space and no intellectual position to which one must agree. Spiritual encounters are possible in this space because central to the experience of parish is a church family who know and love Jesus and who live out the Gospel so that others too may belong and come to believe.

- Implicit in the concept of parish is the notion that the church assumes a pastoral role with everyone in its parish. Whether those people are currently inside or outside the church, our goal is for our relationships to be redemptive. One could say that 'nurturing relationships, seeking a redemptive outcome,' makes an excellent definition of mission!

The gift of boundaries

Parishes have boundaries, and boundaries help us by limiting our scope and focusing our efforts. They bring freedom and clarity.

We can't be everywhere and do everything. Putting a frame around our mission sets us free to invest deeply in one place over time. What does evangelism, creation care and forging *shalom* look like in our place? It is not our responsibility to change the whole world, only to take spiritual responsibility for the place where we are.

Churches who are blind to place must keep asking the questions, 'What should we do?' and, 'Where should we do it?' Without place as a guide, it is difficult to decide between one opportunity and another. We are likely to back the idea of the most persuasive person, or the minister's pet hobbyhorse.

By contrast, when our church family (whatever its size) is rooted in the place where God has planted us, our mission field lies readily to hand. What should we do? We simply ask what evangelism, creation care and forging *shalom* looks like in this community that we are a part of. Where should we do it? Right here of course!

The authors of *The New Parish* say it like this: 'God has given you the gift of limitation and responsibility. Limitations are a sign pointing to your need of the other, while responsibility reveals the other's need of you. What the physical body is to a human person, the parish is to the Body of Christ. The limitation is glorious. It is God's gift enabling you to see and live into your need for others.'[viii]

Our place as a garden

The Father is a gardener (John 15:1), and therefore we can think of every place as a garden. Careful planting, watering and tending within the confines of the garden can turn a barren wasteland into a beautiful, fruitful place that nurtures the soul and is a delight for those who enjoy it.

Gardeners are willing to pour time and effort into making gardens because in their imagination they can picture this bounded place as both beautiful and fruitful before it is so. They also imagine themselves living in it, the garden a reflection of who they are and what they value. People just passing through seldom invest in gardening; those that do intend to, stay.

We were in our mid-twenties when Lynette and I bought our first house. It was small but new, standing in the middle of a quarter-acre of stony, clay soil with not a blade of grass. A home with a yard needs a garden. We were young and proud homeowners, determined to make a fine garden if it killed us—and it nearly did! We invested hundreds of hours making flower beds, raking out stones, and digging in sand and compost. We scrimped and saved to buy trees and shrubs and flowers, and we planted some young fruit trees. We fully expected to still be there when the fruit arrived.

On a recent trip to South Africa we went past our old house to take a look. The houses around where little fuss had been made still looked much the same as ever—but our old property was a green island, the house hemmed in by trees and roses and shrubs on every side. A pine tree we had

> We want for our place what we want for ourselves—to reflect the glory of our Lord Jesus

foolishly planted in the corner of the property now towered above power poles, the wires disappearing through its dense foliage. The trees in the back yard were laden with fruit for others to eat.

What do passers-by think when they see our old property? Surely, they see a place where effort and imagination and resources were spent, a place that was loved. Would we have poured ourselves into someone else's garden like that? Probably not. We did it because it was our home, a reflection of who we are and who we wanted to be.

We need to set our churches free to dream of the real difference they could make where they are planted, not as mission done out of a sense of duty or obligation, but because we want for our place what we want for ourselves— to reflect the glory of our Lord Jesus.

The gift of regular encounters

You may have thought, as I always did, that Jesus stepping into Peter's boat to preach in Luke 5 was a random 'God-moment.' Looking back at Luke 4, however, we see that it was not. This is a watershed moment in a *series* of encounters.

Jesus first met Peter in the synagogue, then at Peter's home where He healed his mother-in-law. Now when He encounters Peter by the shore, it is perfectly natural that Jesus would ask a friend to use his boat. And Peter's life is about to be changed forever!

Relationships flourish through regular encounters

Multiple touches are essential if relationships are to deepen. Relationships grow even quicker when someone is befriended by several people who already have strong relational ties to each other. Being cared for by a group of friends is affirming and encouraging and introduces one to a whole network of relationships.

When we commit to be a blessing to our place, it makes sense that we and our families live as much of our everyday life as possible in our chosen community—that we don't blindly follow the world in chasing after 'the best' in schooling, sports or shopping (which is largely illusory anyway), but rather demonstrate our solidarity with the community by engaging locally. As we together commit to shopping locally, frequenting the local coffee shops, joining the local sports and community clubs, and taking an active interest in local affairs, we enrich our relationships with those who live in our parish. We will also see more of our church family, and our family bonds will deepen.

What does this commitment to a place look like? It is being willing to stand in line a little longer at the supermarket in order to say a few words to the checkout operator you have had past conversation with. Commitment may be costlier—it may even mean that you choose to relocate in order to live with your church family in the parish they serve.

Continuity of relationship helps us model mission

There is natural continuity of relationship in a parish because it is where the church and the people who live in that place both choose to be present. Without a focus on parish, what often passes for mission is a feel-good event with strangers we may not meet again, trusting that the small seed we sow will somehow be watered by someone else and grow. If this is what we are modelling as mission, this is what future generations are going to think mission is.

Real mission is journeying with people to faith. This implies deepening interaction over time. When we ourselves are part of this network of relationships, living alongside both those who seek to woo others to faith and those being wooed, we can see for ourselves what it means to walk alongside those coming to faith. Through vicarious learning and practice we become better skilled; our faith grows, and we are able to pass the baton on to others (Philippians 4:9). This is true discipleship.

Thinking 'parish' helps us reach people in their own space

When we only reach out to affinity groups—the young, the old, those with younger children, businesspeople, the homeless, and so on—we miss seeing their web of natural connections to others. Consequently, we will never touch most of the people in our orbit.

Theologian and author Leslie Newbigin writes, 'The geographical parish can never become irrelevant or marginal . . . the primary sense of neighbourhood must remain primary, because it is here that men and women relate to each other simply as human beings and not in respect of their functions in society.'[ix]

In other words, it is in the neighbourhoods of our parish that we have the possibility of most richly engaging with everyone.

The gift of stability and endurance

When we embrace the idea of being a parish, our sights are set on something more than successfully executing instances of outreach ministry. Through befriending those in our place, we seek to grow a web of relationships that draws outsiders in to experience the family of God and feel the call of Jesus on their hearts.

'Ministry' is often about isolated events on the calendar that quickly come and go. And if we are honest, much outreach ministry is about doing something nice so that people will like us. The church is tempted to place itself in the middle of the story, wanting to be seen as the warm beating heart of the community.

We may be in for a rude awakening. Scripture warns us that when we live an authentic, counter-cultural life we can expect to be misunderstood, have our motivations questioned and our character maligned (2 Timothy 3:12, 1 Peter 3:13-22). As a church family we must decide . . . are we seeking to be popular, or are we seeking to reflect the Kingdom without compromise?

We reflect the Kingdom by being people of truth and grace. Just as we have received grace, we extend it to others. But we also stand upon God's revealed truth. We proclaim that our place can only truly be transformed when it comes under the lordship of Jesus, which is not what those turning from God want to hear. But if we compromise our message, we compromise our purpose and cease being salt and light. It is better to be on the periphery, holding out the word of life, than be at the centre as little more than do-gooders.

Stanley Hauerwas and William Willimon say it well: "The confessing church seeks the visible church, a place, clearly visible in the world, in which people are faithful to their promises, love their enemies, tell the truth, honour the poor, suffer for righteousness and thereby testify to the amazing community-creating power of God. The confessing church has no interest in withdrawing from the world, but it is not surprised when its witness evokes hostility from the world . . . this church knows that its most credible form of witness is the actual creation of a living, breathing, visible community of God."[x]

> Rather than pursue relevance, we should pursue constancy. This requires courage and resilience

Our own need to be liked and be 'cool' often taints our outreach, but we need to see this for what it is. We are not in it to feel better about ourselves. We are here to love our world, whether our community 'likes' us or not. Those who are seeking after God will be drawn to the light through the work of the Holy Spirit, without whom all our efforts are futile.

Rather than pursue relevance, we should pursue constancy. This requires courage and resilience. Resilience is the ability to bounce back from challenging events or overcome obstacles that get in the way of us achieving our goals—and, to keep enduring. Our resilience is rooted in the security of our relationship with God through Jesus, not in the circumstances around us.

This sentiment is echoed by Alan Roxburgh, who agrees that something more than the rush to ministry is called for—something perhaps closer to the Benedictine vow of stability, in which a new monk commits himself to a particular monastery for life.[xi]

Picture a parent who is feeding solids to a baby for the first time. He or she scoops up the food in a spoon and pops it into the baby's mouth. The baby, who is unused to such flavours and textures, spits most of it out again. What does the parent do? Rather than being fazed by the baby's apparent lack of gratitude, he or she continues to persevere until the baby is full. Why? Because the parent is committed to doing the best for the child entrusted to his or her care.

In Revelation 3:8-10, the church in Philadelphia is commended for remaining true to their calling and for not giving up, despite facing headwinds and having little strength. This constancy, resilience and endurance describes our commitment to parish.

Enduring resilience in respect of ministry in and to our place is important both for us and for our neighbours. If I am not sure I will be here tomorrow, why should I invest my life? If my neighbour is unsure that I will be here tomorrow, why should he tell me who he is and what he cares about?[xii]

Real relationships come about through multiple encounters over time and can be bumpy and fraught. But unless we endure and spend the time with people, we will never take our relationships to a deeper level where engaging in redemptive God-conversations becomes possible.

Living as church family embracing a parish with no endpoint is challenging. As the adage goes, you can fool all the people some of the time and some of the people all the time, but you cannot fool all the people all the time. Is our faith more than just talk? As we live transparently with our neighbours, they will discern for themselves whether our love for each other and for our neighbours is able to stand the test of time. There will be reward for our faithful constancy.

PLACE REIMAGINED WITH CHRIST IN IT

Our too-small Christian imagination for what our world could be like with Christ in it has contributed to the world's brokenness.

The richly imagined impact of Christ's lordship recorded in Colossians 1:15-20 sees Him as supreme over all creation (v15) and holding all creation together (v17), with dominion over thrones, kingdoms, rulers and authorities in the unseen world (v16). He is the one through whom God has reconciled everything to Himself and who made peace with everything in heaven and on earth by means of His blood on the cross (v20).

By contrast we have, in the words of Willie James Jennings, 'come to imagine a Christian identity floating above land, landscape, animals, place, and space, leaving such realities to the machinations of capitalistic calculations and the commodity chains of private property.'[xiii]

By agreeing with the powers of this world that the church has no business in these spaces, we fail to imagine a world fully under the lordship of Christ. Without such imagination our prayer, 'Your Kingdom come, Your will be done on earth as it is in heaven' is for something less than heaven intends. We cannot in faith ask for something we cannot imagine.

An individualistic Gospel ungrounded in place is too small. It has seen the church retreat from these vital areas of concern. As light retreats, darkness advances. While the church has been looking the other way, vast global economic and social inequalities have come to exist, coupled with the wholesale destruction of our planet. We have come to see these as secular problems, proof of a world gone mad, but ultimately beyond our control.

We need to do more than make theological pronouncements about these problems. We need to recapture a New Testament appreciation that Christ's lordship over place is part of the Gospel too. As a local church family, our ability to change things half a world away may be limited; but we must lean into a future inspired by our spiritual imagination for how this place where God has planted us can and will be. As we also work to see churches planted in every place, God can use us to make the difference we pray for.

CONCLUSION

Place is frequently overlooked, yet it is so important. God has always sought to embody who He is in community; now the church is His dwelling place. It is this church—family grounded in place—that offers the wider community the experience of being in God's presence. Ongoing exposure provides the necessary context for life transformation. This can only happen when we, the church, are committed to place.

Only a church that has embraced the three corners of *God, People and Place* and has received their place as a gift from God, has the integrity and imagination to be a prophetic voice for the coming Kingdom in which people and place are reconciled under God.

EIGHT WAYS YOUR CHURCH FAMILY CAN EMBRACE PLACE

1. Know where your place is and pledge to it

Ideally, you attend church in a particular community that you can adopt. If you have a church building, it can be a positive trigger for those that pass it every day, reminding them of the good ways you have touched their lives; and it is a place your church family already goes to regularly.

There may be reasons, however, why this is not possible. Perhaps your church is in an industrial or commercial area. It may make sense to choose an area where a significant number of your church family live, or if you have a large church you may have people supporting several local communities through the city. If there is no church building in the place you choose to serve, you need a creative answer to the question, 'How will you be the visible local church to your chosen place?'

However you determine the boundaries of your place or places, the family needs to pledge to establish an ongoing presence there and make relationship-building in this 'parish' a priority. What we say and do together as a church family must reflect that.

2. Confront your roadblocks to embracing place

The first roadblock is *apathy*. Chances are this just won't seem very important to some in your congregation, especially those who see Bible teaching or worship as the church's chief purpose. The change will need to be led from the front by someone who is convinced and convicted that embracing place is part of God's purpose for every church, including yours.

The second roadblock is *customary practice*. If place has no part in your current practice, it has no soil to grow in. Change your practices—or institute new ones—to include a new focus on place.

The third roadblock is *making sense of local church for those who aren't local*. Embracing place means prioritising local relationships as mission. We need to elevate those who live locally, and those that do not live locally need to be willing to make the sacrifice of time and effort to help support local relationships. Allied to this is a challenge to our people to consider moving closer to be in parish. Alternatively, if you have enough people to form a critical core in some other place, why not plant a local church there? If place is important, just how important is it?

3. Discover why things are the way they are

Talk to those embedded in the community who know what is going on. Speak to other church leaders and civic leaders, connect with schools, and talk to the police and social services. Sign up for community emails, and spend time chatting in coffee shops. Find and share articles from the media that pertain to your place. Having a chat with those that have lived in the place a long time can yield gold. Your local council will be running events and providing resources that foster community that you can make good use of.

4. Prayer-walk in your place

Prayer-walking is a wonderful way for our church family to gain a heart of compassion for the people around us. As we walk, we pray a blessing over our place and pray for the needs that God opens our eyes to. I have heard it described as *'praying onsite with insight.'* It invites the Holy Spirit to enter and change our situation. Offering to pray with those we meet is also a powerful way of creating relational God-space. A lot of resources for prayer-walking are available online, including mobile apps.

5. Live more of your life in your chosen place

Where we are able, we should choose relationships over convenience (or saving a few pennies). We support local schools and businesses, do volunteering, or join local sports clubs and community groups in our place as engaging relationship-builders, knowing that relationships lead to conversations that open the door to invitations to experience more of God and the church family.

What would persuade us to relocate so that we could spend more of our life in the place our church family has adopted?

6. Do what you can and invite the community to join you

Whatever you decide to do in your place, remember that we wish to do more than serve—we want to grow relationships. Invite the community to join you in serving and get to know them along the way. Appreciate their help and invite them again next time.

Let's not be afraid of getting behind something initiated by our community. It doesn't need to have our badge on it. The goodwill created by being a good neighbour without seeking glory for ourselves can open more doors than we might first think.

7. Lead in creation care and ethical choices

Caring about place includes stewardship of the environment and being alive to the true cost to others of our consumption. Recycle and compost. Avoid using disposable items destined for landfill. Use glass, not plastic (e.g. communion cups). Serve ethically sourced coffee. Don't run a carwash event without preventing detergent running into stormwater drains. This isn't political correctness; this is treasuring what has been given us as a gift from God.

8. Be cheerleaders for your place

Because this is also *our* place, we never adopt antagonistic 'us and them' language. Our battle is not with our neighbours but with the Evil One who blinds them. We must open our eyes (and the eyes of those around us) to the beauty and potential that exists in our place. Look for God at work and tell the family about it. Encourage and honour community leaders; let everyone who seeks the welfare of your place know that they can count on your support.

i Chris Wright, "Integral Mission and the Great Commission 'The Five Marks of Mission'" (n.d.): 5.

ii Jeremy Linneman, "An Underrated Key for a Fruitful Christian Life: A Rooted Life in a Place," The Gospel Coalition, n.d., 1, www.thegospelcoalition.org/article/underrated-key-christian-life-rooted-life-place

iii Ibid.

iv Quoted by Tim Chester, *Total Church* (London: SPCK Publishing, 2012), 111.

v Ibid.

vi Nicholas Wolterstorff, Gloria Goris Stronks, and Clarence Joldersma, *Educating for Life: Reflections on Christian Teaching and Learning* (Grand Rapids, Michigan: Baker Academic, 2002), 202.

vii Leonard Hjalmarson, *No Home Like Place: A Christian Theology of Place* (CreateSpace Independent Publishing Platform, 2014), 48.

viii Paul Sparks, Tim Soerens, and Dwight J. Friesen, *The New Parish: How Neighborhood Churches Are Transforming Mission, Discipleship and Community* (Westmont, Illinois: InterVarsity Press, 2014), 71.

ix Hjalmarson, *No Home Like Place*, (CreateSpace Independent Publishing Platform, 2014),123.

x Stanley Hauerwas, *Resident Aliens: Life in the Christian Colony* (Nashville, TN: Abingdon Press, 2014), 46–47.

xi www.missions.org.nz/images/pdfs/bulletin/1908_MIB.pdf.

xii Hjalmarson, *No Home Like Place*, 123.

xiii Willie James Jennings, The Christian Imagination: Theology and the Origins of Race (New Haven: Yale University Press, 2011), 293.

4

Clarifying our Mission

Having looked at what it might mean for a church to be a *family* in a *place*, let's turn now to explore what the *mission* of such a church might look and feel like.

WE JOIN GOD IN HIS MISSION

We share our purpose of glorifying God with God Himself. God's ultimate goal is to uphold and display the glory of His own name, not because He is an egomaniac, but because things can only be as they should be when everything is in right relationship to Himself.

Not only is our purpose of glorifying God shared by God Himself, but so is our mission. Our mission is simply to join God in His mission!

Much has been written about the mission of God and the church. A foremost thinker and writer on this subject is Chris Wright. He reduces the five marks of mission adopted by the Anglican Lambeth Conference of Bishops in 1988 into these three areas:

1. *Building the Church* (through evangelism and teaching), bringing people to repentance, faith and obedience as disciples of Jesus Christ. Growing the Kingdom naturally grows the church, as we draw others to the family table.

2. *Serving Society* (through compassion and justice), in response to Jesus sending us 'into the world,' to love and serve, to be salt and light, to do good, and to 'seek the welfare' of the people around us. We need to see the place where God has planted us through God's eyes, and shared ownership of our place makes it *our* mission and not just *my* mission.

3. *Caring for Creation* (through Godly use of the resources of creation along with ecological concern and action), fulfilling the very first 'great commission' given to humanity in Genesis 1 and 2. We need to receive the land as a gift from God and steward it as we should.[i]

These are not three unrelated categories of mission. Wright argues that every aspect of God's mission has the singular purpose of bringing everything under the lordship of Christ, as summed up in Ephesians 1:9-10:

God has now revealed to us his mysterious will regarding Christ—which is to fulfil his own good plan. And this is the plan: At the right time he will bring everything together under the authority of Christ—everything in heaven and on earth.

A little later we learn of God's purpose for His church in all this:

God has put all things under the authority of Christ and has made him head over all things for the benefit of the church. And the church is his body; it is made full and complete by Christ, who fills all things everywhere with himself (Ephesians 1:22-23).

That we are not simply passive as God fulfils His mission in the world is also clearly pointed out later in Ephesians:

God's purpose in all this was to use the church to display his wisdom in its rich variety to all the unseen rulers and authorities in the heavenly places. This was his eternal plan, which he carried out through Christ Jesus our Lord (Ephesians 3:10-11).

Now these are the gifts Christ gave to the church: the apostles, the prophets, the evangelists, and the pastors and teachers. Their responsibility is to equip

God's people to do his work and build up the church, the body of Christ (Ephesians 4:11-12).

Therefore, put on every piece of God's armour so you will be able to resist the enemy in the time of evil. Then after the battle you will still be standing firm (Ephesians 6:13).

As we consider these passages, the first thing to note is that *it is God's plan that we are joining in.* Mission is fundamentally the activity of God and therefore, it will succeed. We join God's mission because it is His purpose for us as His children.

Secondly, we see that God's mission is centred in establishing *the lordship of Jesus over all things.* This is the touchstone of true mission. God's plan is to bring healing and unity to the whole creation by bringing it back into right relationship with Christ.

Thirdly, *the church is both an agent and a beneficiary of God's mission.* Our purpose and mission are so intimately tied to our identity as God's children that we do not get to choose whether we will 'do mission' or not. We cannot have God and reject His mission; neither do we get to choose what we will call mission.

TRUE MISSION GLORIFIES GOD

If our ultimate purpose (our *why*) is to glorify God, this must also be the goal of *what* we do to fulfil that purpose (our mission), and be reflected in *how* we do it (our tactics and methods).

What does God-glorifying mission look like? To bring God glory, mission must also reflect the nature and character of our triune God. We can expect mission to be relational and community-based because this reflects God Himself. God shares His mission with His church, each local expression working together as a body of Christ, part of the whole, one, global body of God's people. Mission is our corporate calling and need not be a lonely enterprise.

Mission is God-focused and is not about us looking and feeling good, but because mission reflects God and fulfils our God-given purpose it should always allow us to be our best selves. We can therefore expect that *how* we do mission should not cause us to inwardly cringe.

Some years ago, we joined the throngs to support our daughter Catherine as she participated in a kids' triathlon. Upon returning to our vehicle, we discovered that someone had seized the opportunity presented by so many parked cars to tuck a bright yellow tract under the windscreen

> We cannot have God and reject His mission; neither do we get to choose what we will call mission

wipers. The front cover proclaimed, 'God loves you—yeah right!' then went on to explain inside that 'God does not love you. In fact, He hates you,' quoting Psalm 5:5 and other Old Testament verses that state how God hates evildoers. The leaflet finished with a 'turn or burn' message. Nowhere on the tract was any indication of who had made it or distributed it.

The tract made me angry. It was a stink bomb tossed into a roomful of unsuspecting people by unknown persons. The tract mishandled Scripture, misrepresented God, and perverted a key component of the Gospel all for the shock value of its title. For every person convicted by its message, dozens more would have been pushed away, having had their negative stereotypes of church confirmed. Yet I could imagine the team that had placed thousands of tracts that day heading back to their base, feeling self-righteous, and high-fiving each other for a job well done.

The people that distributed this tract are no doubt kind and loving and thoughtful towards each other in everyday life, but in mission mode, they became graceless crusaders for truth (even willing to bend the truth to score a point). Mission for them is engaging with the enemy with no need to be gracious. But mission that is neither an authentic reflection of who we are nor of the God that we serve, can never bring glory to God.

OUR MISSION IS TO NURTURE REDEMPTIVE RELATIONSHIPS

Implicit in an understanding of mission that seeks to bring everything together under the lordship of Christ is the key notion of *relationship*. The goal of God's mission is to put everyone and everything back in right relationship with our Redeemer King Jesus for the sake of His glory.

How does God do this? God in His sovereignty can further His mission by drawing people into relationship with Himself through visions, dreams and angelic visitations without our help; but God's mission done through the agency of the church is done humanly through relationship-building, even as we are directed and empowered by the Holy Spirit in the process.

> I propose that we see the heart of church mission as this: the nurturing of redemptive relationships

I propose that we see the heart of church mission as this: *the nurturing of redemptive relationships*. We engage with our world, desiring to see all things restored to right relationship with God. This desire permeates all our relationships, giving them the potential to be redemptive. The relationships we want to see restored to God are primarily interpersonal but include our relationships towards social and political structures and the earth itself.

I believe understanding mission through the lens of nurturing redemptive relationships captures some essential truths:

- '*Nurturing*' speaks to our mindfulness in relationships, and to our motivation of love and care. We turn to our world, not with defensiveness but with openness. We try to see what God sees in everyone we meet. Nurturing also implies a process over time, a perhaps costly journey of faith and hope.

- '*Redemptive*' describes both the quality and the direction of our mission. Our mission is to glorify God by sharing a vision of transformation under our Redeemer King with our world. Therefore, all our relationships, both inside and outside the church, have a trajectory—we want to see people move closer to Jesus and become more like Jesus. It is this trajectory that makes our relationships redemptive. Implicit in every redemptive relationship is the call to keep moving and growing towards God.

- *'Relationships'* lie at the heart of mission. The end-goal of mission is God glorified with everything in right relationship with Him. Our mission is not merely to proclaim the Gospel (which can conceivably be done in non-relational ways), but to make disciples—people relationally engaged with God, their church family and the world. Even our duty of creation care is only achieved through the influence afforded by relationship-building.

I like the fact that when we speak of nurturing redemptive relationships, we demystify mission. Tending relationships is so human we can all understand it. Defining mission this way helps us better understand what we need to do and makes mission doable for everybody.

I also like the fact that the notion of nurturing redemptive relationships ties together God's mission both *inside* and *outside* the church. The church should grow both numerically and spiritually. Numerical growth happens when our redemptive relationships bring outsiders to the family; spiritual growth happens when our relationships with each other are made redemptive through evangelism, teaching, preaching, worship and our body life together as we help shape each other into the image of Christ.

Most compelling of all, I see Jesus nurturing redemptive relationships in the course of His mission on earth. We should pattern our own mission on what He modelled for us.

Jesus nurtured redemptive relationships

In the short space of three years of ministry, Jesus reached many thousands of people and performed many amazing miracles. Yet what He counts as success at the end of His ministry is not these things. In His farewell prayer recorded in John 17, He celebrates the fact that He has kept and nurtured the small band of followers that God has given Him, and through this time together made true disciples of them—followers who recognise His divine authority and are obedient to His word (v6-8).

Jesus' followers weren't chosen from a big pool of people. They didn't audition for the honour of being a disciple. It is possible that they all came from the region of Galilee and at least five of them (Peter, Andrew, James, John and Philip) were from one small village—Bethsaida. They were gathered through ordinary relational networks—the connections of kinship, acquaintance and prior relationship that we all have. They could have come from your town or mine.

The course of Jesus' relationship with Peter illustrates well how ordinary relationships can be made redemptive. We discover in Luke 4 that they attended the Capernaum synagogue together. From there, Jesus was invited to Peter's home, where He healed Peter's mother-in-law. In Luke 5, Jesus is pressed by the crowd and asks Peter if He can preach from his boat. This relationship takes a big step forward as Peter finds himself an audience to Jesus' words of life. But then Jesus reciprocates the favour Peter has just shown Him by taking Him fishing. Having had no success the previous night, Peter now needs help hauling in a net-breaking catch. I see layer upon layer of relationship, each bringing Peter closer to his moment of initial revelation about the true identity of Jesus.

But it doesn't stop there. In the sun of this redemptive relationship, Peter's faith and his understanding of Jesus continue to blossom and grow. It is Peter who steps out of the boat to walk on water, and Peter who first says the words that would be blasphemous if they were not true: 'You are the Messiah, the Son of the Living God' (Matthew 16:16).

Of course, this wasn't only true for Peter, but for all the disciples.

Through her relationship with Jesus, Martha goes from being the one who is too busy to sit and listen, to the only one to express faith in Jesus' ability to raise her brother Lazarus from the dead (John 11:21-27).

Jesus sees Zacchaeus up a tree and knows that spending time together is exactly what this little tax collector needs. Through the course of the evening, Zacchaeus is made a disciple and the injustices he has perpetrated, he pledges to make right (Luke 19:1-10). This is what a redemptive relationship looks like!

There were others to whom Jesus offered the possibility of having a redemptive relationship with Him, only to be rejected. He told the rich young ruler to sell all his possessions, give the money to the poor and follow Him—but instead, he walked away (Mark 10:17-27).

Jesus summed up the heart of mission with these two relational commands: to love the Lord our God with all our heart, mind, soul and strength and to love our neighbour as ourselves (Matthew 22:37-40).

Mission for Jesus happened in the course of everyday life. He performed miracles as the need arose. Life-changing conversations happened on the road and at dinnertime. Jesus looked for opportunities to mingle with the sick and the lost. He accepted invitations to share food and drink. He sometimes asked for help from people just to start a conversation—think of Him asking Peter to use his boat or asking the woman at the well for water.

> Mission done Jesus-style is seldom convenient; it is relational and costly

Mission done Jesus-style is seldom convenient; it is relational and costly. It can be time-consuming, emotionally taxing and includes the possibility of rejection. But it is not simply an occasional duty or obligation; if Jesus had it as His core purpose (Luke 19:10) so must it be for His church family tasked with continuing His work.

Continuity of mission from 'out there' to 'in here'

Of Chris Wright's three aspects of mission, the first is *building the church*. We explored 'being family' first because true mission flows out from our family and brings people back to our family. Our family is mission-critical.

We often speak of church and mission as though they occupy separate spaces. Church is what happens 'in here' with us; mission is what happens 'out there' in the world. We speak of the gathered and the scattered church, and inevitably relegate mission to what happens when we are scattered.

This transcript from a video clip promoting a recent book by two well-known American authors is a case in point:

> 'Sometimes we need to shatter the old, even if it's all we've ever known. For years, many churches have adopted the attractional model, where 'if you build it, they will come.' We sang that it only takes a spark to get a fire going, and our fire was the church. So we break the bank to prop up our buildings and programmes, but the lost still aren't coming. So now, we must live among them—in our neighbourhoods, our schools, our workplaces . . . everywhere.
>
> It will require much more of us. More than friendly smiles for an hour on Sunday. It is about being a missional church—releasing incarnational people into the world. Yet it's also about coming together to refresh, to regroup, to renew our collective calling to change the world. As Jesus encouraged us to imagine like a child, we need to reclaim the courage to be scattered. It's time to explode the status quo, to break free from religion, to discover the adventure of missionary life, to learn how to fly—and together to build a gathered and scattered church.'[ii]

There is a lot to agree with in these words. Being the incarnational people of God indeed requires more than friendly smiles for an hour on Sunday. I detect individualism in the words, but agree that we each need to discover afresh the adventure of living a 'missionary life.' However, the polarising language of 'attractional' and 'missional' church is unfortunate. Why can't church be both attractive and missional?

For these writers and others, when we seek to draw people to church, the direction of the mission arrow points the wrong way. Ministry happens out in the world where we live, work and play, not here in church with us. As church, we gather to scatter; we come to church to 'refresh, regroup and renew our collective calling' for the real work of individual mission in our weekday world. For them, the mission arrow points outward from the church to the world.

I would suggest that the mission arrow goes out from the church but must come back again. We scatter to gather. We go out to connect with the work that God has already begun in the hearts of those who are lost and point them back to the church family. The mission arrow must return to the church family because this is where those who are being saved belong. This is what they are being saved for—a place at the table of the flesh-and-blood family of God, so that they too can begin fulfilling their God-given purpose.

As we saw in chapter one, the gathered church is called to be a witness to the world. The purpose of the gathered church is to glorify God and to be a living demonstration of the power of the Gospel to its neighbours—to be a 'Kingdom hotspot,' if you will. On my own, I can show how a citizen of the Kingdom behaves and I can demonstrate my allegiance to the King, but to truly model the Kingdom takes all of us in community.

Mission doesn't end when 'they' come through the door; coming to salvation is just the beginning of our spiritual journey. God wants more than our salvation—He seeks our perfection. More than that, He desires our recruitment to His mission.

So, there is continuity of mission from 'out there' to 'in here,' and the pathway created by God's family nurturing redemptive relationships together naturally leads back to the family. This is how God grows His church; He grows us numerically by adding new believers, and He grows us spiritually through our participation in the fellowship of believers, through teaching and exhortation, and through faith-growing mission.

Redemptive relationships form the pathway to faith

How are outsiders to faith going to find their way into our church? Few will find their own way there; most must be wooed through love, friendship and invitation.

Having interviewed two thousand post-moderns who had come to faith, authors Don Everts and Doug Schaupp, in their excellent little book *I*

Once Was Lost, uncover the five thresholds to conversion that outsiders must cross.[iii]

They must move:

1. *From distrust to trust.* Somewhere along the line, they learned to trust a Christian.

2. *From complacent to curious.* Through the work of the Holy Spirit and their association with a Christian they became curious about Jesus.

3. *From being closed to change to being open to change in their life.* Through the work of the Holy Spirit and association with Christian friends they became open to examining their personal lives.

4. *From meandering to seeking.* Through the work of the Holy Spirit and association with Christian friends they move from asking questions to seeking answers.

5. *They cross the threshold of the Kingdom.* Through the work of the Holy Spirit and the support of Christian friends they come to faith.

What we discover is that the journey to faith is organic. It takes time and doesn't follow straight lines. The Christians who support this journey are joining God who is already at work in the hearts of those who are not yet believers. Only the Holy Spirit can bring someone to repentance and conversion. The job of the Christian is to offer the redemptive relationships that keep bringing seekers back to the pathway by making faith credible and desirable.

What makes a relationship redemptive?

Any relationship that glorifies God by pointing to Him is redemptive.

In such a relationship, I commit to seeking God's best for the other person and am prayerfully alive to opportunities presented by the Spirit of God over time to woo my friend closer to Jesus through words, deeds and answers to prayer. We offer this friendship because we see the other person through the eyes of Jesus, not just as they are but as they might be. We imagine them as Spirit-filled followers of Jesus and in faith we believe that it can be so.

We are also being redemptive when we work with others to bring about justice, mercy and reconciliation—this is patient, difficult work which often cuts across vested self-interest. Some, like Queen Esther, may be raised by God to a position of influence in order that they might use their relationships to intervene for the good of the wider community (Esther 4:14).

All our redemptive relationships are patterned on Jesus. Whatever the circumstances, we should always remain kind, respectful and relational— our mission should be an expression of our best selves and not something we are later ashamed of. We can all participate in mission as Jesus' body on earth and still be our authentic selves.

Jesus-inspired mission looks less like shouting on a street corner or tracts on a windscreen and more like meals and conversations at home. It is less about controlling conversations and more about authentic caring. It carries the possibility that we will be hurt—this is part of what it means to be fully human in mission. Yet we can draw comfort and encouragement from the fact that we are on this exciting adventure together as family.

Mission that is squeezed into a time box or a method box makes mission the focus, rather than the relationship. It can be forced and unnatural, making both us and the target of our mission awkward and uncomfortable. We are not excluded from using

> It is less about controlling conversations and more about authentic caring

tools and resources in the process, but relational mission happens on God's timetable and goes in the direction and at the pace needed by our friend.

THE EVERYDAY MISSION OF THE CHURCH FAMILY

Most church members have the reasonable expectation that their church will help them fulfil their missional purpose both in church and in the world.

However, what church usually offers them is an opportunity to serve in a limited number of highly specific boxes. These boxes are programme opportunities. Most of these programmes happen out of sight of the congregation at another time and place, making it difficult to discern which role is a good match. Some have mysterious names that obscure their purpose; others can immediately be discounted because they serve a group that excludes the opportunity-seeking member; and yet others are at a place and time that makes them inaccessible.

The result is that very few find their 'mission box,' but in truth no-one is really looking for a box at all. Deep down what we all want is a life without boxes. What we long for is a purpose and mission that makes sense of all of life.

The model of missional church we are exploring embraces our whole life. Our personal mission is to take every opportunity to nurture redemptive relationships in our world so that we might build the church, seek the welfare of the place where God has planted us and care for God's creation. The mission of our church family is to help us do so. Sometimes we play a leading role, at other times we play a supporting role. Both roles are equally necessary when we are doing mission together.

Every Christian is responsible for the full spectrum of mission, both in the church and in the world, as opportunities arise for each of us in God's timing. If God owns it all, His family must own it all too. We don't get to choose which part of mission we will and won't do for God. Our giftings help shape the *role* we play in God's mission but not its *scope*. I cannot, for instance, say 'I am doing my bit as an evangelist' and so justify turning a blind eye to societal hurt. Jesus says to all of us in Matthew 25:31-46 that we can show compassion for the poor and needy or we can go to hell.

> Deep down what we all want is a life without boxes

This then is the big-picture view of how the everyday mission of the church family works: as a Spirit-filled believer we befriend those who we encounter in our world, seeking through example and conversation to draw them closer to Jesus. We are encouraged to do so through the support and accountability offered by our church family. Through hospitality and invitation, we seek to grow their relational network by introducing them to Christian friends. Together we then draw them to the church family table, where their coming has been anticipated and will be celebrated. There they experience authentic Christian family, unambiguously hear the Gospel, and also hear the first-hand stories of the power of God in changing lives. Convicted by the Holy Spirit they repent and become Christ-followers too, thereby growing the family which in turn grows them and supports them in mission.

The scenario described above is not likely to happen in this picture-perfect way. Real life and imperfect people will cause detours from the ideal path. However, this simple missional blueprint can work in all places at all times. The Acts 2 account of how God added numbers to the early church reflects this blueprint, and in some parts of the world it is the only way to do mission. Where the Christian faith is persecuted, the church cannot do mission with billboards and flyers and fanfare. Relationship and trust with an individual must be built first; then the prospect is introduced to a few other Christian friends who help assess the risk of inviting this outsider to the larger gathering.

In this model every church family member has a purpose and role to play. Real-world mentoring and discipleship (and accountability too) are built in as we participate together and learn from each other. Our faith grows as our expectancy that God will move in the hearts and lives of the unsaved is proved correct.

The implication for our mission as a church family is clear. The member's role is not merely to support the church in its mission—our relationships *are* the mission, and we need our church family to support us!

PROGRAMMES AND EVENTS ARE NO SUBSTITUTE FOR REDEMPTIVE RELATIONSHIPS

The idea that the mission of the local church is to support the redemptive relationships of its members strikes most as novel. More often than not, when asked about mission, church leaders will begin by listing the special events and programmes they run for the benefit of the wider community outside of their regular (usually Sunday) service.

Such programmes, targeting children or young mothers or immigrants or those in need of parenting, budgeting or marriage advice, have a place when they also serve those in church, but when they are our sole expression of mission, they are a very imperfect platform.

- *They can only ever reach a tiny proportion of the population.* If we rely solely on such programmes, it is as though we are peering at our community through a peephole. The highly specific 'need filter' winnows our potential mission field to a few random stalks of grain and hides from view the natural network of relationships our prospects have with others.

- *Our programmes can only include a small number from our congregation.* If we believe that mission is a key part of the spiritual formation of those in our church, then it is unfortunate that our programmes can each only employ a few of them. And we cannot simply multiply the number and diversity of programmes to increase engagement—our buildings have only so many spaces, there are only a limited amount of available booking hours in a week, and the budget can only stretch so far.

- *Our community programmes bring hardly anyone to church.* The number one concern of church leaders running outreach programmes is the lack of intersection between the programmes and church on Sunday. The reality is that precious few of the people who attend our midweek programmes end up in Sunday church with us. I wonder if part of the problem is that the organised, logistical people needed to successfully build and run a serving programme are not necessarily the organic, relational people who will take the time needed to woo outsiders to church.

- *Our programmes largely focus on meeting the needs of strangers* instead of building redemptive relationships with those God has already brought into the lives of our church family. Everyone in your church and mine is already in relationship with at least one other person who has not yet come to faith. But instead of fostering the relationships we already have, we pour our efforts into trying to form new relationships with people we don't yet know by offering them a service.

I am not anti-programmes. There is a place for programmes and events in the mission of the church. Programmes that meet the needs of the family and are open to including outsiders can aid the family mission of the church by helping us build relationships inside and outside the church. But the focus of mission should be the nurturing of relationships, not the provision of a service.

> The focus of mission should be the nurturing of relationships, not the provision of a service

Why is there nearly universal acceptance of the fact that needs-based programmes are the best way for churches to reach the people in our world? If we are off-course, we need to take time to understand how we arrived here in the first place.

Our journey to frustration

Here is my purely personal experience of how trends in local mission and community outreach have evolved over the past forty years or so; I wonder if your journey parallels mine?

I grew up in a corner of the evangelical church that was leery of anything that smacked of the 'social' Gospel, based in works and not in faith. What people needed was the message of the Gospel so they could be saved. What was the point of good works? Why try to simply make people more comfortable on their journey to hell?.

But that was not the viewpoint that prevailed. Few evangelical churches in New Zealand today would disagree that the Gospel is a matter of both demonstration and proclamation, that good news and good deeds need to go hand in hand.

Somewhere along the way, the concept of *needs-based evangelism* arose. The basic idea is that you discover a felt need in the community you are targeting with your evangelistic efforts, and that in meeting that need you create opportunities for the Gospel.

Take, for example, a soup kitchen. Our target community might be the homeless or out-of-work; their felt need is a warm meal, and Christians can introduce the Gospel into this situation by requiring that the recipients of the soup hear a Gospel presentation as a precondition of receiving the soup.

For some, there is an element of discomfort in the sketch I have just given. Should we really compel unwilling listeners to listen to our message just to receive the help we offer? Shouldn't we be offering warm bowls of soup to the hungry just because it's the right thing to do?

A new wave of thinking emerged. Steve Sjogren, founder of the Vineyard Church in Cincinnati, calls it 'servant evangelism,'[iv] borrowing a phrase from Mother Teresa. He believed that small things done with great love could change the world, that acts of kindness can help build bridges to the Gospel by giving a taste of what the Kingdom is like, thus creating opportunities for conversations about faith. Soon, the phenomenon of 'random acts of kindness' arose. Whether it was giving away free cans of cola at the traffic lights or cleaning toilets in the mall, servant evangelism reinforced a simple formula: find a need and meet it in God's name.

What this new thinking did was to uncouple the demonstration of the Gospel from its proclamation. 'Good deeds' became part of a longer game, evangelistically. Their purpose was to create a climate more conducive to receiving the proclaimed Gospel; however, it was no longer urgent (or even appropriate) that the message be proclaimed at every encounter. I would consider that this is still the ruling paradigm for most church-based mission work today.

While there is certainly merit bound up in all of this, this thinking can become a trap. When the focus is on meeting needs now and deferring evangelism for later, we can end up building needs-based service programmes for the community that never effectively get to the Gospel.

We believe we were saved to serve, so we build service organisations

I am not for a moment suggesting that it is wrong for churches to meet practical needs in ministering to their community. However, it is building relationships rather than meeting needs that should be the guiding principle of our missional engagement. When our mantra is 'see a need, meet a need,' we naturally begin thinking of the most efficient and cost-effective ways of meeting the need at hand. Too many churches are effectively meeting needs in ways that are unlikely to ever lead to conversations about Christ because they are centred in service-delivery rather than relationship.

I know of a church that cancelled the morning service in order to serve at a local school. That Sunday they did a wonderful job of cleaning, repairs and gardening and even enjoyed a time of worship together. The job got done— but there wasn't a single unchurched person on site. Instead of inviting the school parents and staff to come and work alongside them shoulder-to-shoulder and so grow relationships, they chose to do it all themselves. What a missed opportunity!

As I write this, it is the time of year for churches up and down the country to put on alternative Halloween events. Some will do this well, but many of these events will consist of people standing in queues for a free sausage, ice-cream, or jump on the bouncy castle. Personal conversations will not just be difficult—they will be impossible.

Of course, it is possible for these 'goodwill touches' to be part of a broader strategy that may lead to relationships and Gospel-drenched conversations. All I know is that I seldom hear churches articulate an intentional, credible plan for bringing it about.

I wonder if deep down some of us are thinking, 'If we are saved to serve and we are serving, God is pleased. Good has been done. People coming to faith would be wonderful, but that is the gravy. Our acts of service are the meat and potatoes.'

That we are called to serve is beyond question, but let's take our template for service from Jesus. Yes, Jesus was a servant—but His self-sacrifice served a greater purpose.

The most-quoted passages of Scripture that point to the servanthood of Jesus also reference His mission:

> *For even the Son of Man came not to be served but to serve others and to give his life as a ransom for many (Mark 10:45).*
>
> *Though he was God, he did not think of equality with God as something to cling to. Instead, he gave up his divine privileges; he took the humble position of a slave and was born as a human being. When he appeared in human form, he humbled himself in obedience to God and died a criminal's death on a cross. Therefore, God elevated him to the place of highest honour and gave him the name above all other names, that at the name of Jesus every knee should bow, in heaven and on earth and under the earth, and every tongue declare that Jesus Christ is Lord, to the glory of God the Father (Philippians 2:6-11).*

In short, Jesus served to save, and so should we. We serve the world because we want to see all things come under the lordship of Christ. Only Jesus can truly change a life. Our best efforts for others, if they don't point to Jesus, will come to nothing.

What is the best thing that ever happened to you? Surely, it was finding Jesus! We do not truly love our neighbour if we are keeping Jesus from them, no matter how joyfully and professionally we serve them.

We spin our lack of success

We use programme attendance figures to describe how many we are reaching rather than how many Gospel conversations we are having. We cling to the stories of how we made someone's day better but have few stories of how we changed the course of someone's life for eternity.

We hide our lack of success behind statements such as these:

- *'The programme is their experience of church.'* Does our programme really satisfy the criteria of being church? Central to the practice of church is the fellowship of believers, including teaching, prayer and the sacraments (if Acts 2 is to be our guide). If this is happening, then your programmes really are planting churches—and we all want to hear your story!

- *'It's not about bums on seats.'* Of course not, but it does beg the question: what is it about? Surely it is about growing the Kingdom and seeing folk brought into the fellowship of faith, or else why are we doing it? If we are seeing people come to faith in our church programme who are then finding a spiritual home elsewhere (so that their bums end up on another church's seats), we need to get to the 'bottom' of the problem as to why our church is repelling new believers.

- *'At least they are getting used to being in our building!'* There is a prevalent belief that people don't come to church because they are weirded out by the space in which we do church. Familiarity with the space reduces hurdles to coming to church.

Let me say that if the spaces in which we gather are a barrier to people coming to church then some remodelling may be in order. But chances are, that isn't the problem. For most people, using space in a building on Wednesdays creates no sense of connection to another group that happens to use the building on Sunday. What will get them to our regular church service, is their friendships with real live people who warmly invite them to come.

We persist because programmes give us cover

It may bother us that by some measures our programmes and events are not serving us very well. On the other hand, by different measures they serve us very well indeed.

- *There is comfort in all being in the same boat.* Despite the shortcomings of programme-based outreach, if that is what everyone else is also doing then we are in good company!

- *Programmes give our church something to feel good about.* Every church knows that it should be doing something to reach out beyond its walls. This programme is what we do. Box ticked.

- *Programmes provide opportunities to serve (for some).* They need leaders and teams and volunteers who can contribute to the life of the church by running the programme.

- *Programmes give our church something it can put its name on.* All the flyers, posters, business cards, websites and social media pages relating to our programmes have our church name on it. It's a great way to grow brand awareness (and help your church look like a happening place).

- *Programmes make life convenient for us.* Programmes are simple and unmessy. They happen between certain hours on certain days. The rest of our life is partitioned off and insulated from the ministry event.

- *Programmes give us control.* We know what's going to happen and what's not going to happen. Our agenda, our rules.

- *Programmes help us feel safe.* When we are providing a service that others are grateful to receive, things couldn't be more pleasant. There is no risk of personal rejection. I believe it is our fear of rejection more than anything else that drives us to settle for offering a service rather than risking a relationship by talking about Jesus. This may be why we put our best effort into trying to reach people we don't yet know, rather than doing more with the people we already do.

WE MUST EMBRACE THE RADICAL ALTERNATIVE

If we agree that the mission-as-programme paradigm falls short, we have to consider the alternative—the paradigm of mission-centred church, where mission is our core purpose and involves everyone. When this is true, we gather not as passive congregants but as active missioners. We go to Scripture to hear it speak to our mission; and our worship is fuelled by what we see and experience of a faithful God at work in the world.

It is our fear of rejection that drives us to settle for offering a service rather than risking a relationship

Such a church understands we are there to mutually nurture relationships that will bring us and others closer to Jesus. Instead of recruiting members to serve our programmes, we create programmes that support the relational mission of all our members. This means spending a lot more time talking and engaging with each other and a lot less time passively present. We discuss the things that matter most and are taught how to listen with understanding so that we can exhort one another to faith and good deeds.

We mutually support and encourage each family member's redemptive relationships with outsiders by demonstrating that we care. We keep track, we pray, and we offer our own friendship as a support to their friend. Our church gatherings are missional. We invite our friends to share an authentic experience of church family with us and we rejoice when they come. We faithfully proclaim the Gospel and challenge newcomers to join us in the mission.

As we have seen, this is what the baby church in Acts did. It appears that inviting others to experience the hospitality of the family of God first-hand was central to how the early church reached out to its community (Acts 2:42-47). It is the premise of this book that it can and should be so again.

Letting the change touch what happens on Sunday

We may be afraid of what such a change of paradigm might mean for our church, especially if it touches the Sunday service. There is a lot at stake. It is tempting to present this as a good idea for a different gathering, such as our church small groups, so that nothing need change about Sundays. However, Sunday is when we have the majority of the church present in one place. Unless we change Sundays, nothing will change. Our flagship event signals our core values and beliefs. It is our choice to either shape it around participation by our active missioners, or to prepare a programme for our passive consumers.

When we shape it around our missioners at least we are also modelling discipleship to our passive attenders; but when we shape it for our passive consumers, we reduce the time and opportunity for true body life for everyone. The mission and spiritual formation so

Unless we change Sundays, nothing will change

necessary to our faith becomes something that must happen somewhere else. For most of those sitting around us on Sunday, that other moment is not going to happen.

The time we spend together on Sunday is precious and short. We need to make the time count by maximising our body life together. This not only helps us; it also allows those we will be inviting to come to experience the church being family. Let's put fear aside and look at the possibilities before us with the eye of faith. In the next chapter we will explore a practical model that makes sense of the part that both the individual and the church as an organisation must play in fulfilling the mission of the church.

But first we must confront the elephant in the room—that the mission I am describing has no box. It has no clear boundaries and is likely to be time-hungry. Can an approach that requires so much of our already-busy church members ever work?

WHEN WE ARE 'TOO BUSY'

As I have sat with pastors talking to them about intentional, relational mission supported by the whole church family in the places God has planted them, most resonate with what I'm saying. Some however say to me, 'The people in my church are so busy, I'm just not sure we will have a lot of people willing to take this on.'

As Christian leaders we need to push back against the notion that we might be too busy to fulfil God's mission for His church. Here is why:

Being a family on a mission is not just another thing to do

The first important thing to note is that we are describing 'whole of life' mission. Rather than trying to fit mission into our lives, we are re-orienting our lives around mission. We are mindful of nurturing redemptive relationships throughout our day wherever we are.

The time we spend with those we are befriending together with others from our church family as we pursue our mission together is not wasted, empty time. It is necessary time that God is using to grow us and others so that we become more like Jesus. What more fruitful way could we have spent that time?

We have never had more discretionary time

We all have twenty-four hours in a day, and each of us is using that time somehow. To that extent all of us are 'busy.'

Despite what we may think, we do have a great deal of discretionary time at our disposal. In fact, one recent survey of 32,000 participants concluded that almost every demographic has around five hours of discretionary time a day—that is, time not spent:

- working in the labour market

- pursuing formal education

- working around the home, taking care of children and family, cooking, cleaning, shopping, etc.

- in self-care, such as eating and sleeping. [v]

So what do we do with our five hours?

Well, typically, *around three hours is devoted to screen time*, twenty minutes to sport and exercise and the remaining 1 hour and 40 minutes is spent on other things like:

- socialising (including social media)

- entertainment

- volunteering

- religious activities

- education for personal interest

- travel.

What we discover is that there is plenty of scope for most of us if we choose to use our time differently!

Workaholism

There are certainly those who seem to work every hour of the day that God gives them, but the same study shows that it is the richest demographic that is sacrificing leisure time rather than the poorest. This sacrifice is not out of necessity, even if workaholics dress it up that way. They enjoy working and the benefits they derive from it more than non-work activities, and they pay the price in relationships. We need to confront workaholism as an addiction that robs us of time to help fulfil God's larger purpose for our lives.

The basis of our problem is spiritual

The values of our society run counter to the values of the Kingdom of which Jesus is the King. The hallmarks of our culture are not contentment, simple living, contemplation of God or making time for family, friends and neighbours. These values should be in evidence everywhere in the church, but to the extent that they are absent we should be insisting upon them as the mark of true discipleship.

This is not unreasonable. I meet people all the time who have chosen to work fewer hours, live more humbly, and trust God more about their security in their old age in order to be salt and light in their community now. These are real disciples who have chosen to take Jesus at His word when He exhorts us stop worrying about tomorrow, our food, and our clothes, and instead seek His Kingdom.

You can't build God's Kingdom on a foundation of hedonism and consumerism. As the famous German poet Johann Wolfgang von Goethe once said (tongue in cheek, no doubt), 'If you start your buttons from the wrong hole, you won't have a hole for your last button.'[vi] As leaders in the church, we need to help our people get their buttons right by setting the bar where Jesus Himself set it. We cannot accommodate worldly values. We cannot live for self and Christ. We have to die to self and take up our cross daily. This is the cost of discipleship. Those unwilling to pay the price cannot be a disciple—it is as simple as that.

We must call out the idolatries that rob us of time

When last did you preach against busyness? J. D. Greear says, 'Busyness isn't just uncomfortable; it's dangerous. There are few things as damaging—and potentially soul-destroying, as busyness.' He also quotes Blaise Pascal, noting that busyness sends more people to hell than unbelief.[vii]

Why is this so? It is because busyness gives us no time for nurturing the soul, for hearing the still voice of God. We fill our lives with what we see as urgent, and neglect what is important.

Spiritual formation takes the eternal perspective. Our foundation is Christ—not philosophy, self-reliance, human morality, ethics, financial security, power, self-interest or self-empowerment. The Kingdom mindset focuses on what will last, not on what passes away. If you are a church leader and your people are chasing the wind and not finding time to build the Kingdom, it is your duty to call it out.

We must speak out against the systemic evil that robs the poorest of time

Not everyone in our congregation is working themselves to death by choice. There are families having to work long hours at more than one job just to get by. There are principles of greed and inequality built into our society that favour the rich and disadvantage the poor. Those who have to work on weekends and holidays just to support their family are probably not spending quality time with God, family or their neighbours. In short, they are being forced to live a life that is not as God intended.

For the church, acquiescing to this evil system is a dereliction of duty. Rather than merely lamenting how the world has changed, we should be speaking out for things like a living wage and reasonable work hours. This is not just 'political'; this impacts the fabric of our society both inside and outside the church and shapes our lives and future. The mission of the church is also to serve society by calling for justice and compassion where it is needed.

CONCLUSION

In this chapter, I challenged a popular paradigm of programme-based church mission and made a case for being a church family on a mission that needs the participation of everyone. Rather than recruiting members to serve our programmes, we must support the relational mission of all our members.

The locus of mission is not just *out there* in the world, but also *in here* as we invite outsiders to share our family table and experience for themselves the mutual ministry of the body of Christ. Instead of a needs-based approach to mission we should see our role as nurturing redemptive relationships.

We noted too that relational ministry done Jesus' way is costly and requires our all. We need to be prepared to embrace change in how we do church if we are to follow this more holistic paradigm of missional church. We also need to address the cultural values that come to church with us which are alien to the Kingdom of God if we are truly to be disciples of Jesus.

> Relational ministry done Jesus' way is costly and requires our all

In the next chapter we will explore a practical model that brings together our personal role and our church's role as we fulfil God's mission for our church together.

---

[i] Chris Wright, "Integral Mission and the Great Commission 'The Five Marks of Mission'" (n.d.): 5.

[ii] "The Gathered and Scattered Church," www.youtube.com/watch?v=ebJY0kyPFCM.

[iii] Don Everts and Doug Schaupp, *I Once Was Lost: What Postmodern Skeptics Taught Us About Their Path to Jesus*, First Edition (Downers Grove, Ill: IVP Books, 2008), 23–24.

[iv] "Servant Evangelism," *Steve Sjogren Blog*, n.d., www.stevesjogren.com/servant-evangelism/.

[v] Roland Sturm, "Free Time and Physical Activity Among Americans 15 Years or Older: Cross-Sectional Analysis of the American Time Use Survey," *Preventing Chronic Disease* 16 (2019).

[vi] Quoted in Joshua Choonmin Kang and Richard J. Foster, *Deep-Rooted in Christ: The Way of Transformation* (Downers Grove, Ill: IVP Books, 2007), 39.

[vii] "4 Ways to Win the Battle Against Busyness | J. D. Grear," *The Gospel Coalition*, www.thegospelcoalition.org/article/4-ways-to-win-the-battle-against-busyness/.

5

Being on Mission Together

A s a kid, did you ever play 'telephone' with two cans and a piece of string? It took two people each holding a can to keep the string taut, and only then did the 'telephone' work. It was remarkably effective, even over long distances. What made it fun was the cooperative nature of the game—and wondering what silly thing would be said next!

Mission too is meant to be cooperative. As we have already seen, the biblical emphasis is on mission done together, rather than by individuals operating as lone rangers. We may each be first-responders as we minister the love of Christ to those we befriend in our personal world, but we need to feel that taut string back to our church

> Just as it takes a village to raise a child, it takes a church family to raise a disciple

family, knowing that they care and that we can turn to them for prayer, active support and advice.

Just as it takes a village to raise a child, it takes a church family to raise a disciple. My role as first-responder should only be temporary. I need to wrap other Christian relationships around my seeking friend as soon as possible to increase the number of redemptive relationships this friend has in his or her life. As this friend is drawn into my circle of Christian friends, the spiritual gifts God has given each of them can all come into operation to accelerate my friend's progress to the cross and onward to a lifetime of discipleship as part of the family of Jesus.

If I were to diagram the picture I have just painted for you, this is what it might look like:

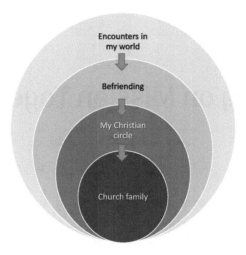

This strategy looks simple enough, but a common mistake is to place the greatest emphasis on the individual's mission in his or her world. This may seem logical; even in my diagram the arrows begin on the outer edge and move inward.

However, I would probably not be on the frontline thinking like a missioner at all if I were not part of a team for whom mission is a normal part of culture and practice. To be effective as a missioner in my world, I must believe it is necessary and important, I need a game plan and I need the support and accountability of like-minded people I respect. This team is my mission-focused church family.

What is more, if we are to successfully draw not-yet-believers from the outer circle to the inner circle where we hope they will come to faith and in turn come to embrace their own sense of mission, we need the cooperation and support of our church family at every step. Our mission is too big for us to us to achieve all on our own. Mission's centre of gravity is the mission-minded, Spirit-filled church family.

What then must be true for our church if we are to be a family in a place for whom nurturing redemptive relationships together is cultural, practical, and inclusive of everyone?

A CULTURE OF BEING A FAMILY ON A MISSION

Along our spiritual journey every one of us has accrued understandings of church that shape what we think the purpose of church is and how it should be 'done.' These understandings, reinforced by our practices and the language we use, form the culture of our church.

Our own church plant, *church@onetwosix*, is only four years old as I write, and was begun with pioneering volunteers from five different denominations who committed to being part of the church plant for only one year. You will appreciate how different this is to planting a church out of an existing church where there are prior relationships and the culture of the mother church to build on.

The method we used is probably not recommended in any church-planting manual, but from a small base we have seen fifty percent growth year on year and were recently incorporated as a Baptist fellowship. I think one of the reasons our church plant has worked is precisely because we had to form new relationships and build a new culture together. We had to talk explicitly about what our mission and our culture would be. We had to go through all the usual stages of group development: forming, storming, norming and performing.[i]

We began with a group of motivated people of goodwill, each of whom brought their own prior understandings of what church should be and do. As trust grew and opinions were expressed, some of these prior understandings were challenged. We lost some people who had come to 'do mission' and didn't see the need to form family first. But as we persisted with our model of *church family in a place on a mission together*, we formed a new identity with new language and behaviours that now make this description true for us.

Last Sunday we took just a couple of minutes to ask the question, 'What do you appreciate about *church@onetwosix*?' The person at the whiteboard struggled to keep up!

Here is what was top of people's minds:

- Sense of family

- Everyone is a participant

- Freedom to talk; discussion time around the table

- Love for one another

- Everyone is appreciated

- Informal and relaxed with no sense of hierarchy

- Our tagline, 'Come Hungry,' which points to the physical and spiritual meal that anyone can come and enjoy every Sunday

- The stories from our family members of how God is using them in the world

- Our practical sermons and heartfelt worship

- Chocolate!

As a leader in the church I might wish that other important ideas also made the list, but this is an honest snapshot of the culture of our church while it is still in formation, and our shared understanding of what is important to this church family.

The members of your church also share an understanding of what is centrally important to them—your church's *raison d'etre*. What would your people say it is?

Some churches are tempted to think of worship or Bible-teaching as the centrally important thing that we must do as church, but if the purpose of church is to glorify God by bringing all things under the lordship of Christ, then it must be our mission that is centrally important. Satisfying intellectual and emotional needs is not enough. To fulfil our purpose together we need to be primed for action, for mutual co-missioning. As important as worship and Bible-teaching are, they do not lead to spiritual growth unless we are also exercising faith as missioners in the world. Hebrews 11 makes it clear that it is a lived-out faith that is pleasing to God, and James 2:14-26 very bluntly tells us that 'faith that does not lead to action cannot save us.'

When Bible-teaching and worship are an integral part of mission as they should be, the result is fervour and spiritual growth; but we can let these good things work against mission by allowing them to become an end in themselves. They can crowd mission out and push it to the periphery where it must find expression either in a narrow church-sponsored mission box that happens at another time and place or in the random, infrequent, unfocussed, unsupported actions of our members.

If mission is not what binds us, the existing culture of our church can sabotage our efforts to be a family on a mission together. Changing the culture of any organisation is a big deal, and one which we will turn to in the next chapter. For now, let me share from my own experience the three pillars that are needed to build a culture that supports being a family on a mission together.

Pillar 1: The way we talk about ourselves

It is how we see our world that determines our experience of it—and we do not all see and experience the world the same way. We all routinely ignore most of what goes on around us as we filter for what is meaningful to us; we cannot assume we all share the same framework of meaning.

This is why language is so important. Words create worlds. Our words can create a framework of meaning which we can all share. We can turn the light on for people who never saw it that way before. What seemed ordinary or even pointless can become important and precious when its

Words not only make sense of our present experience but can create future worlds for us to step into

place within the whole is understood. Words not only make sense of our present experience but can create future worlds for us to step into by creating a picture or a map that points the way.

At *church@onetwosix* we began by talking about being a church family in Point Chevalier on a mission together before it was true. We kept it up until the language became our common language, descriptive of who we really are.

We call our meal on Sundays a family meal, and the inclusion of communion ties into that. As we consider our mission, we speak of inviting others to share our family table. When we transition to talk about what God is doing in and through our family, we call it 'family time.' We celebrate milestones like birthdays and anniversaries as a reminder too that we are family.

We regularly talk and pray about Point Chevalier as the place where God has planted us to be a blessing to our neighbours. We pray for the new neighbours who will be moving in next door as Housing New Zealand builds twenty-two new apartments on the site adjacent to us. We imagine what it will be like having maybe twice as many to dinner, and what we will do to manage the influx.

We speak of mission using the language of invitation, and the first question we ask in family time is, who invited somebody this week? We are clear that our primary mission is to those God has already brought into our life and that success looks like inviting them to take another step with us.

We have found that as we are consistent in how we speak about ourselves and our mission, the language is picked up and used by our members. Naming something is the first necessary step in making it real.

Pillar 2: A clearly understood pathway for mission

'Mission' is a somewhat mysterious concept for most people. Do I need to hear or feel a special prompt from God? Does my paying for a stranger's coffee count? How about leaving tracts on park benches?

I don't believe that just anything counts as mission. None of the above are worthy strategies to promote to our church. God's mission already has a direction and purpose and we don't need any special, individual prompting to be part of it. Unless we are nurturing redemptive relationships with a view to bringing all things under the lordship of Christ, what we are doing is a sideshow. Somehow, without excluding the possibility that God may prompt one to do something out of the ordinary, we need to demystify mission and give it clear tracks to run on, or we will never be able to coalesce around mission as a church.

The nested circles diagram above has been seen by our *church@onetwosix* family many times. Our regulars understand that the heart of our mission is to form relationships that lead people to Jesus—and that our church family wants to be a part of that process.

We have come up with a mission strategy for our church that everyone can understand:

> **'Our mission is to invite those we befriend to join our church family so that, in the power of the Holy Spirit, we can bring restoration and healing to our place and God's world together.'**

What this may lack in theological rigour it makes up for in clarity. Mission defined this way can no longer be thought of as either mysterious or random. Rather, it becomes the ordinary human process of making friends, being a truthful witness to the work of Jesus in our lives and then wrapping other Christian friends around our not-yet-saved friends, trusting that they too will become part of the family.

While we take every opportunity to evangelise, to bring *shalom* to our place, and to be advocates for creation care, we recognise that relationship-building is the heart of all outward-facing mission. When we confront others with the claims of the Gospel it is not just to make the world a better place by changing outward behaviour; we also want the Gospel to be redemptive in their lives, drawing them to the One who can effect an inner transformation so that they can be adopted into the family of God.

Better than diagrams for helping our family understand our mission is seeing it play out in the lives of real people they have come to know. We can point out those whose lives have been touched and changed by our church family and we remind the church of their stories.

Several of our members are champion inviters, and through word of mouth it has become known that we are a place to come for a free meal, so we expect to see first-time guests every Sunday. Many first-timers will choose to leave after they have eaten, but those who return are welcomed back by the family and their story quickly becomes known. It becomes harder to eat and run; they stay for family time, the worship, and the message. As we

> By doing mission together we increase the number of Christian relationships in the lives of the seekers we know

discuss the implications of the Gospel for our lives at our tables afterwards, they get to express whatever faith, fears and doubts they might have. As they open up to someone, they are likely to be spontaneously prayed for; and they will leave feeling lighter for having shared their burden.

After a while they may begin turning to the family for support in fighting addictions and dealing with oppressive anger and guilt in their lives. We invite them into our homes, and we visit them in theirs; we journey with them on Messenger and Facebook. When called upon, we serve as their advocates in government departments and the justice system.

Even if we do it imperfectly, we are taking 'living out the Gospel' as a church family seriously. Are people coming to faith and being baptised? Of course they are, because there is power in the Gospel!

By doing mission together we increase the number of Christian relationships in the lives of the seekers we know. This multiplies the conversations, prayers, good advice, and words from Scripture that the Holy Spirit can use to draw them to repentance. Throughout their journey to faith, the seeker experiences the family they will need to support them on the other side of their faith decision.

What we will call mission can never be fuzzy or nebulous. If our people are not clear on what counts or what is expected of them, we cannot blame them for doing nothing.

Pillar 3: Letting the family shine

If we are after a culture where the whole church family is on a mission together, it takes more than a leader up front declaring it to be so. Every member of the family needs to be empowered and made responsible for making this statement true.

In many churches the microphone is held by a select few who speak on behalf of everyone and in effect tell a passive congregation what to think and do. This is not how a healthy family operates. If we are talking 'family business,' every family member should get to have their say. We must let go of the microphone, trusting that the upsides will outweigh the downsides (and there will be some).

One of the upsides of handing over the mic is that we get to better know who is in the room and what they can contribute to the family. At *church@onetwosix* we all know who in our congregation is bold for the Lord and has the gift of evangelism, or encouragement, or practical service, because we have had opportunity to hear their passion, see them in action and experience their gifting first-hand.

We create several opportunities at every Sunday gathering for the giftings of those who are following Jesus to shine through.

Our Sunday gatherings commence with *communion,* and we shoulder-tap members of the congregation who are demonstrating faithfulness to lead it. For some, this is their first experience of public speaking. We provide them with a briefing document beforehand to assist them in leading this roughly five-minute segment, but we encourage them to share from the heart. Not everyone is a great orator, but some have led with such assurance that we see their potential for preaching and will seek to equip them for this role. Others get more and more exuberant as they share the Gospel message at the heart of communion, and we see them for the evangelists they are. Not only does the wide spectrum of folk leading add interest to our gathering, but the insight it gives us into the hearts of our people is remarkable.

For those who have become core to our fellowship, *our meal* is about creating a hospitable space where we take an interest in others and are alert to each other's needs. At the tables our evangelists shine, as do our pray-ers and mercy-givers—and of course, those with the gift of hospitality are in their element! As the mix of people at each table changes week by week, over the course of time everyone gets to see what we each 'bring to the table.'

Family sharing time is only ever facilitated by the core pastoral team because we don't know what is coming, and sometimes things are said and situations arise that need rescuing! During this time, we have a roving microphone that comes to the tables as folk indicate they want to share. The prompt questions we use to lead this time are:

- Who invited someone this week? (We celebrate inviting, whether they come or not).

- Did you learn something good during the mealtime conversations?

- What did you learn from reading the Bible this week?

- Did something big happen to you this week? Did your faith make a difference?

We hear some amazing God stories of what happened through the week, but we have also been rocked by instances of betrayal and injustice that have touched our family. Those of us fighting addictions sometimes have setbacks. We stop and pray as we hear these stories. We also hear spontaneous public confessions of guilt and repentance, which I have never experienced before—it seems to be the result of both feeling safe and having the Spirit move. We also have to practise forbearance with a few tiresome folk who love having the microphone and a captive audience, and we have had to confront someone who seems to be a compulsive liar. A real family then!

Our family sharing time helps model the behaviour we expect of an imperfect yet outward-focused family wanting to please Jesus. We experience praise, joyfulness, brokenness, and disarming transparency. More than any other church I have been in, this is one that knows how weak and poor it is but is learning to lean on each other and on the Lord. There is something beautiful about that.

After the message we discuss at our tables how the message applies to us, and a spokesperson feeds back to the rest of the room the most important learnings from their table. We hear insights and gems of application that the preacher never thought of. The simple act of taking the time to ask, 'What did we learn today?' crystallises the message for ourselves and increases the likelihood that what was said will not be forgotten as soon as we leave the room. We want to accelerate the process of making disciples, not make it harder—and we want to make the precious few hours we spend together count for as much as possible.

> We want to accelerate the process of making disciples, not make it harder—and we want the precious few hours we spend together to count for as much as possible

THE PRACTICE AND STRUCTURES OF A FAMILY ON A MISSION

You will appreciate that our culture and our practice are closely tied together. Our practice is what we do to support the culture we want, requiring that we structure our spaces and allocate time appropriately to make our practice of being a family on a mission possible.

Structuring our time

If relational mission is to be the heart of our church (rather than our liturgy, our preaching, or our worship in song) and if our church is to be a family on a mission, we have to allocate an appropriate amount of time for relationship-building. We cannot simply introduce three minutes of meet-

and-greet into a 'regular' service and think that will do the job. Relationships take time and cannot be rushed.

At *church@onetwosix* we spend two hours together on a Sunday evening. The first 45 minutes we have communion, eat and converse at our tables. The next 20-25 minutes we have family time and notices. Thereafter we sing just two songs, and we raise the roof doing it. We then hand around Bibles and chocolate and have a message that takes 20-25 minutes, followed by 10-15 minutes of discussion around our tables. We close with a benediction relevant to the evening we have had. After packing away tables and chairs and cleaning up in the kitchen, we are done.

I don't think we leave out anything essential that a 'regular' church might do, yet there is perhaps only twenty minutes out of two hours during which it might be rude to have a conversation with the person next to you. We don't just choose to call ourselves a family; we spend the time to make it real. Let me stress again that this isn't just time cosily spent with old friends—the time is also being spent missionally with friends and seekers who are still on the outside looking in. When we are being family, we are simultaneously on mission.

Through the week our other events—our Connect Group, walking group, craft and games night, and our prayer meeting—all flow out of being family on Sundays. For some churches it is the other way round. They hope that they can do enough to be family outside of their Sunday event (e.g. small groups) so that family is assumed when they gather on Sunday to focus on something else. In reality, however, most churches engage far fewer of their people through the week than on Sunday. What a waste not to build the best of what a small group has to offer into the Sunday service!

Creating a conducive environment

Right now, your Sunday space is set up to best support what is core for you on Sundays. Auditoriums with fixed seating are great if the main action is going to be on a stage or platform and little to no interaction between attendees is required. However, to be a family on a mission requires the space to be configured differently.

You will have experienced the difficulty of having conversations for any length of time when seated in immovable rows of chairs all facing forward. 'Get into groups and have a chat with the people around you' involves firstly overcoming the social awkwardness of unexpectedly moving from private space cued by the seating arrangement to social space where I must now interact. We must then deal with the fact that those in the row in front must either twist around or spend the next few minutes kneeling on their seats. It is uncomfortable in every sense and not conducive to growing relationships. The room screams that what you are doing is not normal for the space.

In the early days of our church plant we began with a meal in the hall with the tables set out banquet style. After the meal we would move into the lounge and sit around the room on couches and beanbags. When we outgrew the lounge area, we began migrating from dinner in the hall to the larger space at the other end of the building, carrying the couches and beanbags with us. One day we asked ourselves, 'why not do everything in one space?'

What we settled on is setting out our tables in the largest room in a herringbone formation and having our entire service at the tables. The tables create zones of intimacy for conversation and discussion, and it is easy for folk to move their chairs to get a comfortable view of the front when needed. It works perfectly for us.

To aid conversations and getting to know one another, everyone wears a nametag. Newcomers and visitors get a tag as soon as they arrive. These nametags are clipped to a board that is put out each Sunday for easy retrieval. Your name on a nametag board says, 'you belong here.'

To enhance our sense of family, we hang portraits of our *church@onetwosix* family down the halls of our church. Visitors to our space often spend time looking at our portraits, and when a new one is added it is quickly noticed! Not everyone with their picture on the wall has yet come to faith, but all have demonstrated belonging by behaving like a host, rather than a guest. Baptism is our marker for becoming one of the core family of faith and only baptised believers may have roles of leadership, but the portraits have become a socially important mark of belonging.

> Not everyone with their picture on the wall has yet come to faith, but all have demonstrated belonging by behaving like a host, rather than a guest

Church has also become a place where we share produce, donated bread, and second-hand clothing. This was all initiated by our members and we are happy to encourage it because it fosters our sense of community and creates more opportunities for our people to serve.

Every church's situation is unique and there will be natural constraints on what your church can do to enhance the space it has to make it more suited to the purpose of being a family on a mission—it will require careful thought and consideration to ensure that your space does not work against your desired outcome.

Programmes for us *and* others

Our church does not have many resources, and everyone in leadership is a volunteer. The programmes that we implement outside of the Sunday service, therefore, need to tie in closely to our understanding of our mission. Programmes that our people will attend and would love to invite their friends to are ideal. Programmes for the real or imagined needs of people we don't know and where no natural pathway exists for relationship-building are not considered.

We are not, for example, presently about to start a programme for young mums with pre-schoolers, even though there are plenty in our suburb. Excellent as such programmes are, they would serve no-one in our church, since right now none of our people have young children of their own. If we went ahead and began a programme for mums with pre-schoolers, who would run it? And where would be the natural relational connections back to our church? We could pressure folk into putting on a programme, but they would make better use of their time pursuing the natural relationships they already have in their world. What we do have are many single, lonely people. Our craft and games night meets a real need for our family, and it is a fun event that they can easily invite a friend to.

To reach out to our place we have created a recognisable brand called 'I love Pt. Chev.'—with our own logo, stickers, T-shirts and Facebook page. We periodically invite our neighbours to come and help clean plastic off the local beach or join us in some other community activity. We like these sorts of shoulder-to-shoulder opportunities, where we get to meet people while serving together.

When we have all the resources and the other person has all the need, the relationship is unequal, and pride and resentment can be a barrier to our words. When both parties are serving, however, we are on the same side of the fence and there is an easy equality of relationship that makes others more open to our overtures of friendship. Then we can invite them back to serve with us again next time and build on the relationship!

We have also had eco-friendly carwashes at our place where we invite folk in for a coffee and a chat. We have had a family-friendly 'Bunco' night with prizes donated by local businesses. These activities all give the people of Point Chevalier an opportunity to meet our church family and are events to which we can also invite those we are befriending in our world to introduce them to the wider circle of believers.

We love the Alpha course.[ii] This programme (and others like it) is one of the few 'off the shelf' options available to the New Zealand church that helps us reach out to the people we already know. The rhythm of Alpha, with its ethos of hospitality and being a safe place to ask questions, fits perfectly with our church culture. We run Alpha periodically as part of our regular church service, and its content is also excellent grounding for those who are young in their faith.

OUR SUPPORT FOR THE MISSION OF EACH FAMILY MEMBER

We have painted a picture of a church family that sends missioners into the world and then, through words and hospitality, blesses those who return with them to the family table, with an experience of the Gospel. Can the church family also practically support our members in the frontline of mission in their individual worlds, where they must stand alone?

We can resource and equip each other

We do not set the bar to be a successful missioner very high, because it needs to be doable by everyone. We ask our people to be their authentic Christian selves, to offer friendship to those God brings across their path, and to try and introduce their new friends to their Christian circle, usually through an invitation to a social or church event. Consequently, the two base skills everyone needs are: knowing how to build a relationship with someone; and, knowing how to invite them to something.

The best resource we have found that teaches skills in building a redemptive relationship with a new friend, is Doug Pollock's book *God Space*.[iii] Doug explains how, by using 'Noticing,' 'Serving,' 'Listening,' and 'Wondering questions,' we can naturally lead into spiritual conversations. I highly recommend working through this book with your church.

We also teach 'inviting skills' through our *Love Your Neighbour* ministry, where, in a two-hour workshop, we confront our fears about inviting someone to a church event. We teach that success is inviting someone in the power of the Holy Spirit and leaving the results to God. We then demonstrate how we deal with a 'No,' 'Maybe' and 'Yes,' and we get

> Everyone needs to know how to build a relationship with someone and how to invite them to something

everyone to role-play making invitations. Taking our church through this workshop as part of a special Sunday service has given everyone at *church@onetwosix* a newfound confidence.

We find that offering to pray for the needs of our friends is a simple, straightforward way to introduce our faith into a growing friendship. We offer our family a little booklet that they can give away called *Trypraying*.[iv] It is a Gospel-based seven-day prayer experiment for those who are trying prayer for the first time. After praying for our friends, we can say, 'Would you be interested in learning how to pray for yourself? This little booklet will tell you how.'

For those growing in boldness and wanting to clearly articulate the Gospel for themselves and others, we want a Gospel outline that not only shows the way of salvation but also answers the question, 'What is God's purpose for me once I'm saved?'

We have developed our own five-point summary of that answer:

1. God created us to live in harmonious relationship with Him, with others and with creation (Revelation 21:1-7).

2. Our self-centredness (sin) has broken our relationship with God and hurts ourselves, others and our world (Romans 3:23, James 3:16).

3. By paying the penalty for our sin Jesus made it possible for us to have our relationship with God restored forever (John 1:12, Romans 6:22-23).

4. When we commit ourselves to follow Jesus and receive His forgiveness the Holy Spirit gives us the power to live as God intended (1 John 1:9, Galatians 5:16).

5. God includes us in His family where we have a part to play. Together we also help restore the world to Him (1 Corinthians 5:19-21).

We can support each other through accountability

Our church-plant had only been going a few months when we tried to introduce the idea of Life Transformation Groups, a term I believe originated with Neil Cole, author of *Organic Church*.[v] The idea flopped at the time because we were too new to each other, and our commitment to the church and to one other was not yet strong enough.

We have recently reintroduced the idea and have shaped the concept to best fit our culture of being a family on a mission. It is still early days, but the enthusiasm for what we are calling 'Growth Groups' is exciting.

A Growth Group has two or three members of the same gender who agree to meet for no longer than one hour a week and work through a set outline based around Scripture, prayer and mutual accountability. The purpose of our Growth Groups is to enable our church family members to motivate and support each other so that we each grow spiritually and personally and live out our purpose. As we see success and multiply each group, over time we expect that our church will grow numerically too.

Everyone takes turns at leading the group and asking the questions. The goal is for the group to be mutual, accountable, and safe. As the questions are asked week by week, we also want to keep continuity with what each person has shared in the past. Here is the outline we are using:

Regarding God:

- How have you sensed God's presence in your life during this past week?

- Have you received a specific answer to your prayers?

- What have you learned about God in reading the Bible this past week and how will you better obey Him?

Regarding Ourselves:

- What area of your life do you feel God most wants to change? Are you taking specific steps to make those changes?

- What good habit do you feel God wants to form in your life? Have you taken specific steps to develop that habit?

- How can we help keep you accountable for seeing this through? How else can we pray for you?

Regarding Others:

- To whom have you shown God's love during this past week?

- How have you progressed your relationships with unbelievers this week? How can this group support you in your mission?

- Have you invited anyone to meet others in your church family socially? Have you invited anyone to share a meal with us at *church@onetwosix?*

(Respond in prayer to what was shared in each section)

This accountability to trusted others brings an edge to our Christian life and mission which also accelerates our growth as disciples of Jesus.

We can support each other's redemptive relationships

Our Growth Groups reinforce the idea that we will be available when called upon to share in the befriending of each other's new friends, understanding that the more of us this new friend gets to know, the faster they will cross the five thresholds to faith we mentioned in chapter four.

Supporting each other's redemptive relationships can be woven into the natural course of our day.

This is beautifully illustrated by the following story, recorded by *Love Your Neighbour* a few years ago:

> *Jacqui Caetano is an evangelist at heart. Some years ago, Jacqui decided to walk to keep fit instead of going to the gym. After a few days she had the thought, 'Why not invite others to go walking with me?' She did a simple letterbox drop and numbers grew each day, until a large number were involved, even if they didn't walk every day. The morning walk was known as 'The March of the Penguins' because it started on Penguin Drive on the North Shore and progressed to the beach.*
>
> *Jacqui quickly drew other Christians around her to intentionally take time to chat with other residents on the walk. 'We share the stories of our lives, we tell*

of answered prayer, and we pray out loud for each other,' Jacqui told us at the time. 'The ladies who are not Christians are welcomed and included, but the Christians openly live out their faith.'

Walking companions soon became good friends, and their social interaction grew. They began spending time in each other's homes. These walking friends attended baby showers, watched movies together in the home theatre of a member of their group, and even went around to one person's house to celebrate the purchase of a new coffee machine.

Thanks to Jacqui and her Christian friends, some of those from the walking group came to faith. Jacqui felt especially privileged to lead the baptism of a Thai Buddhist friend who came walking with her. After Jacqui had used her as an interpreter to explain the Gospel to another woman, she had told Jacqui that she wanted to receive Jesus too!

A MODEL FOR CHURCH FAMILY DOING MISSION TOGETHER

I have used the story of our church-plant to illustrate the core ideas in this chapter. Ours is an easy example because it was founded on the principles this book aims to share and therefore what we do naturally 'fits.'

There are, however, principles embedded in our story from which we can construct a model for how *any* church can be a family in a place on a mission together. With a model to work from, any church can begin to make progress towards this goal—and measure their progress.

In the following diagram, I have attempted to pull together all the elements needed to become the kind of church where everyone is on mission and growing in their faith:

My mission helps grow the church family

Church family supports my mission

The family table
- Introduce new friends to the family
- Be their guide and interpreter
- Include them in family time
- Help them stay engaged

Mixing church friends & seeking friends
- Personal hospitality – invite my new friends to meet my Christian friends
- Invite my new friends to programmes and events provided by church

Being a disciple
- Nurture personal walk with the Lord
- Desire to see all things under the lordship of Christ
- Love and befriend my neighbour, speaking of the hope I have

Gathered church
Springboard and landing place for mission

Merge space
Wrapping Christian relationships around not-yet-Christian friends

The individual missioner
Support, personal responsibility

Culture
- Authentic
- Whole gospel
- Relational
- Inclusive
- Everyone is on mission

Modelling & opportunities
- Programmes that serve us and others
- Opportunities to serve society and care for creation that can include neighbours
- Invitational events (e.g. Alpha)

Personal equipping
- Belonging to a growth group for accountability and support
- Skills training
- Encouragement and celebration

The diagram explained

In this model, the cycle of mission has the gathered church family both as springboard for mission and its destination. A church that is growing through repeating this cycle is a spiritual movement.

The cycle is divided into two halves—the left half describes how the church family corporately reaches out to support each individual missioner, while the right half describes how each individual missioner is then able to build the church by bringing others to the family table.

Mission happens in three contexts, denoted by the three central double-sided arrows. The arrows are double-sided because each of the contexts has both a corporate and an individual dimension. The three contexts are: the gathered church, 'merge space,' and the individual missioner.

Starting at the top left of the diagram and working in an anti-clockwise direction, we see that gathered church serves the mission of its members by establishing a culture that makes it normal for everyone to be a missioner. The hallmarks of this culture are that it is authentic, relational, inclusive, and embracing of the whole Gospel—and that it is a family on a mission together.

Corporately, the church then aids the goal of introducing seekers to the church family by creating 'merge spaces' where we merge the two worlds together. In these merge spaces we are enabled to initiate redemptive relationships with the neighbours in our place and share the relationships we are nurturing in our personal worlds with others in the church family. These merge spaces include programmes that can serve both the church family and outsiders, the opportunities we support or create to serve our place and care for the environment, and specific invitational events such as Alpha. As church family members participate in these corporate opportunities, they can learn from the experience and gifting of others as they see missional behaviour and conversation modelled for them.

Completing the first half-circle, the church family plays a part in the personal equipping of each individual member for their role as missioner. Small accountability groups support and encourage the spiritual growth and mission of each member. The church must also teach the practical skills of nurturing relationships, inviting to 'merge space' opportunities, and sharing one's own faith journey with others.

Continuing along the outer arrow, we move to the right-hand side of the cycle where the emphasis is now on the responsibility of the individual member to be a missioner who grows the church family. The left-hand side of the cycle is corporate and programmatic; the right-hand side is more opportunistic and flows from our everyday discipleship. We must each nurture our personal walk with the Lord, desiring to see all things under His lordship. Then, as we go about doing the things we care about, God brings certain people into our world. Our role is to love and befriend them whilst remaining our authentic, Christian selves.

Continuing up the arrow, we want to increase the number of redemptive Christian relationships our seeking friends have in their lives. This has the potential to greatly accelerate their progress towards Jesus and salvation. To this end we are able to use the programmatic 'merge space' opportunities that our church regularly provides, but we should also create our own organic 'merge spaces.' Through personal hospitality and invitation, we can creatively help our church friends and our seeking friends to mingle.

Having befriended him or her together, it is a natural step to invite our new friend to meet the rest of the family gathered at church. There they will be expected, welcomed, and accepted. They will continue to hear the Gospel and have their questions answered. This experience of the family table is a foretaste of the Kingdom to come. God by His Spirit will bring many to repentance and build them into His family to help repeat the cycle.

MAKING THIS TRUE FOR OUR CHURCH

The first step in shaping our church towards being a planted church family on a mission together, is to take stock of our present reality.

Diagnostic checklist

The following diagnostic checklist identifies 21 attributes of such a church, divided under three headings: our culture, our structure and practice, and our support of each member as missioner. How well is our church doing as a planted family on a mission together? Give each statement a score:

1 – Not true of us　　　　　3 – Often true of us
2 – Sometimes true of us　　4 – Always true of us

A. Our culture	Score
We are authentic (demonstrating love, humility and brokenness without pretence)	
Our language reflects that we are a family on a mission together	
Everyone has a family role to play	
We are inclusive, making time for relationships	
We see and talk about the power of the gospel to change people and the world	
Our homes are open to each other and visiting each other is commonplace	
We expect and celebrate new people on Sunday	
Sub-total	

B. Our structures and practice	Score
Our church space is structured to make relationship-building easy	
We have a clear pathway for mission that everyone understands	
We focus on reaching the place where God has planted our church	
We create opportunities to serve alongside our neighbours	
We care about and pray for the issues facing our local community	
We encourage our people to invite friends to our regular church programmes	
We run invitational events like Alpha that help outsiders experience the church family	
Sub-total	

C. Our support of each member as missioner	Score
We encourage everyone to be in a small accountability/discipleship group	
We equip our people in the art of invitation	
We equip our people to be able to talk about their faith	
We publicly celebrate their stories of friendships made	
We regularly ask each other about our personal walk with the Lord	
We share resources with each other that enrich our spiritual lives	
We encourage making friends of seekers together	
Sub-total	
Total score	

This checklist of attributes can provide a present-day scorecard for your church that will highlight both areas of strength to build from and blind spots that need attention. Identify your weakest area. Was it A, B or C? Within your weakest area, what activity, project or initiative could you and your community undertake to boost your score? Why not try that and score yourselves again each year, taking definitive steps towards stronger family dynamics?

This checklist can serve as a tool for measuring your church's progress over time if you regularly return to it. I recommend that you make a record of your church's score today, then revisit it each year to measure your progress. You may want to send it to yourself in the form of an email and flag it for your attention twelve months from now.

This list could also be the basis for a church-wide conversation about the kind of church you want to be and the steps you will take to get there. Conversations can be big (where we come to grips with the whole vision), or they could be about just one attribute on the list that you want to do well. Such conversations are necessary to effect change, as we shall see in the next chapter.

Does your church have the will to change? Change is uncomfortable, and the discomfort will only be endured if we desire a different future strongly enough. You may already know deep down that no matter how much you love your church and the people in it, they will not follow you on this journey.

If you are strongly drawn to the picture this book paints of church, and your current church is not likely to change, I challenge you to embrace the possibility that God wants you to plant a new church with a new DNA. Planting a church can be done by volunteers and doesn't require a theological degree. If you give yourself the freedom to fail, you will find it can be a faith adventure that is challenging, exhilarating and even fun. We will discuss what this might look like in the last chapter.

[i] "Tuckman's Stages of Group Development," *Wikipedia*

[ii] www.alpha.org

[iii] Group Publishing, *God Space: Where Spiritual Conversations Happen Naturally* (Loveland, CO: LifeTree, 2009).

[iv] "Trypraying," n.d., www.trypraying.co.uk

[v] Neil Cole, *Organic Church: Growing Faith Where Life Happens* (John Wiley & Sons, 2005).

6

Embracing Change for a Hopeful Future

How does the local church achieve its purpose of glorifying God in the world? We do so by fulfilling our three-fold mission of building the church (spiritually and numerically), serving society, and practising creation care.

All of mission is characterised by our desire to be agents of reconciliation as we nurture redemptive relationships, drawing others to Jesus and including them at the table of God's family. When this is true, God can use us as He brings all things under the lordship of Christ in the place He has planted us. Such a church is more than an institution—it becomes a movement infused with passion, purpose and growth, that makes disciples and shows them how to live out their purpose.

Right now, despite all the good things that are true for your church and mine, there is probably a gap between this ideal and the reality on the ground. How do we narrow this gap and become more the church God wants us to be? The answer is both obvious and uncomfortable. We have to start doing some important things we are missing and stop doing whatever unhelpful things are blocking us. In short, we need to embrace change.

UNSERIOUS CHURCH

My dad used to tell a joke that always raised a chuckle in church circles.

> 'The new minister preaches his first sermon and it is brilliant! His new parishioners congratulate him on an excellent message; it is all they can talk about that week. They can hardly wait to hear him preach again.

> 'The next Sunday he climbs into the pulpit and preaches the identical message. His parishioners find this odd, but since it was such an exceptionally good sermon, they forgive him. However, when he preaches it a third time, consternation ensues, and so they buttonhole him about it. "When you start putting this message into practice, I will preach another!" he tells them.'

What makes this tale amusing? It is the absurdity of knowing that the minister is absolutely right—*and* that his expectation is utterly unrealistic!

In the West it seems that, whatever is preached or taught, changing our behaviour as a consequence is entirely optional—even for good churchgoers. There is no live expectation that we will come back any different the following Sunday; there is therefore no mutual accountability for change. This makes being and doing church fundamentally *unserious*.

Imagine a weight loss group where week after week the trainer lectures about the effects of obesity and how dieting will change your life, yet there is no requirement that the members actually diet, or even step on the scales. Would you believe that club was serious about losing weight?

In this example, there may be a lot of good, healthy behaviour happening. The group may be welcoming and friendly. Lifelong friendships are possibly being made. It may be a safe place. The people are likely well-informed and know the latest nutritional information. They may be making their payments promptly and be very encouraging of their trainer.

What this group is not doing, however, is focusing on the critical behaviours necessary to help them meet their big picture goal of losing weight. In this example, we all know what the needed behaviours are—they need to set weight goals, adopt an eating plan, and measure progress by regularly weighing themselves. Additionally, they need to encourage each other and hold each other accountable for those right behaviours.

Spiritual formation is about changing behaviour

There is a direct parallel between our imagined weight loss group and the church.

The church is called to be a place where our attitudes, behaviours and practices are shaped so that we grow to be more and more like Jesus and become increasingly useful for the sake of the Kingdom. To grow is to change. Ephesians 4:11-13 says:

> *Now these are the gifts Christ gave to the church: the apostles, the prophets, the evangelists, and the pastors and teachers. Their responsibility is to equip God's people to do his work and build up the church, the body of Christ. This will continue until we all come to such unity in our faith and knowledge of God's Son that we will be mature in the Lord, measuring up to the full and complete standard of Christ.*

Spiritual formation is about changing our behaviour. Spiritually mature people behave differently to spiritually immature people, not only in matters of personal piety but in doing God's work. The more Christ-like we grow, the more we act in ways that are counter-cultural to the world around us. It is this very difference that makes us salt and light in the world.

Our temptation as leaders, however, is to avoid introducing the accountability that is required to ensure that our people keep growing both in personal holiness and in missional effectiveness. Perhaps we fear creating a graceless, performance-based church culture. I do wonder if what we mostly fear is that imposing

> The church is called to be a place where our attitudes, behaviours and practices are shaped so that we grow to be more like Jesus

any kind of expectation will cause people to leave, taking their wallets with them. Yet this kind of accountability within a safe, grace-filled and trusted circle is what every true disciple craves. Growth is life-giving. It meets a hunger placed inside us by the Holy Spirit Himself. By not requiring growth, we can unwittingly create an environment where change is discouraged, and it is our best people who will eventually move on.

If we want to be a church that is serious about fulfilling our purpose in the world, then, like that weight loss group, we have to check that we are doing what is necessary and important to reach our goal.

In every God-fearing, Bible-believing church there will be many good things that we can point to as evidence of life, hope, and blessing. The problem is, when confronted with our blind spots and shortcomings, it is tempting to point to those good things and say in effect, 'This is the kind of church we are and good things happen here, so we don't need to change.' Facing and embracing uncomfortable truths can, however, become a pivotal moment, setting us on a new trajectory. It is not a bad church that is willing to embrace change, but a good one.

We ended the last chapter with a checklist of attributes that are true for a church in a place on a mission together. To what extent are these attributes true for your church today? Are there existing practices that may even be working against you?

Choosing to take stock of our present situation is a courageous first step, but it is only a first step. It is what happens next that will determine if our church remains on a path to growth.

WHAT KIND OF LEADER IS NEEDED FOR CHANGE?

We all know models of church where it appears the church exists to bring about the vision and goals of its leader. The leader is considered 'anointed of God' like some Old Testament prophet, priest or king, and no decision of consequence is made without their say-so. Through force of personality, or status conferred by the hierarchy, such leaders lead and their flock must follow—with the sheep analogy seeming particularly apt.

The model of church I have been sharing is also biblical yet is quite at odds with this picture. If church is to be a family on a mission together where everyone is using their giftings for the common cause, then *every* member must be able to contribute to (and shape) the church family and its direction.

So how do we lead change in an organisation where direction comes not only from above, but from those around the table? By perceiving leadership as a team role, which can be shared around. In this model, the leaders act as facilitators to help the whole family shine. Even in this context, leaders are essential for change, but they do it through dialogue and consensus-building . . . and through strategic intervention.

CHANGE IS NEVER EASY

Change is essential to growth, yet resistance to change is human and normal and affects every organisation. However, there are reasons why bringing about change in the church context is especially difficult.

For one thing, the church has its roots in antiquity. We are part of an unbroken line that stretches back two thousand years. We tend to draw comfort from the essential unchanging nature of church that gives us continuity with those who have gone before and those who will follow us. We are conscious that we worship an unchanging God in a changing world. We are the very definition of *conservative*: averse to change or innovation and holding traditional values.

> A church is not a just an organisation, it also meets the personal and social needs of its members

We are consequently loath to touch our model of church, even if we recognise that the shift in society around us calls for a different way of doing mission. The separation of church and mission into the two spheres of 'church gathered' and 'church scattered' is a convenient way of keeping the church model we love while still trying to practise new ways of doing mission in the world outside our walls. It neatly ducks the question posed by this book of whether we need to change our model and restructure how we do church in order to be truly missional.

But there is another strong factor at play too. A church is not just an organisation, it also meets the personal and social needs of its members. The behaviour it requires is highly collaborative, with great value placed on being 'nice.' We have done consultation work in churches where everyone we speak to can name an issue, yet these individuals feel helpless to facilitate change and continue to conform because they believe it is what everyone else wants. We can call this 'sociological resistance to change.'

A church's default setting is the culture of values, customs and unspoken rules that everyone abides by. We naturally and unconsciously revert to this default setting unless we publicly address the elephant in the room and agree to be mutually accountable for the change.

Love Your Neighbour learned this truth the hard way. For years we ran training courses for community-facing ministry leaders, trying to equip them to lead change for greater missional engagement in their home churches. What we discovered was that what we were asking them to do was practically impossible. The rest of the church had not been on the training course and were still on their default setting; without the authority and opportunity to address systemic issues and share their learnings, how could these ministry leaders catalyse change in their church? The result was that the benefit of the training seldom extended past their own ministry bubble.

A FAMILY CONVERSATION ABOUT THE CHANGE WE WANT

For real change to happen it must involve the whole church. It is essential that the church family have a conversation about who we are and what we want, because for real change to happen we need to grow consensus around why change is needed and what is at stake.

I am speaking of a real conversation, not a church meeting. A real conversation only happens when people feel safe and are given the opportunity to look each other in the eye and speak their heart. There must be space and time for everyone to be heard, including those who are shy and timid. A church meeting with agendas and rules of order and resolutions, with people in rows and the microphone dominated by those with big personalities and strong opinions, is the wrong forum altogether for a real and inclusive meeting of minds.

In their book *Conversations Worth Having*[i] the authors describe what a 'conversation worth having' looks like. It is a rich conversation that is:

- *Meaningful*—it is about something important that we all care about

- *Mutually engaging*—it is a conversation we can all contribute to

- *Generative*—it is geared to generate information, ideas and new possibilities

- *Uplifting and energising*

- *Positive*

- *Productive*—it has an outcome.

A great way to lead into a family-wide conversation worth having is to go on a journey of discovery together as a church. Rick Warren's *40 Days of Purpose*[ii] is a great example of material that does this. *Love Your Neighbour* has developed the *Redemptive Family* church series[iii] which similarly seeks, through a combination of daily devotional readings, weekly surveys, sermons and small group studies, to share a fresh vision of church based on the principles of this book. Our experience is that when a shared vision is compelling enough, our people are more than willing to sacrifice the time needed to talk about it.

> A real conversation only happens when people feel safe and are given the opportunity to look each other in the eye and speak their heart

What might a church-wide conversation look like? Over the past decade we have facilitated a great number of church conversations using these guidelines:

- Invite people to attend and give them a compelling reason to be there, but don't force them. Those who care will turn up. The right people are always those who are in the room.

- Create a relaxed, friendly space. Set up informal groupings around tables or in zones.

- Come to answer a question that everyone agrees is important. The more powerful the question, the greater the benefit from having the discussion.

- Do not have a pre-determined outcome in mind. This is an act of bad faith.

- Find creative ways to encourage the participation of everyone. Get people to move around. Engage their imagination. Don't be boring!

- Give feedback afterwards so that the outcome is clear.

- Do something about it—make a change in consequence.

Bringing in an outside party to help facilitate the conversation can be very helpful, even if it is not essential. Tools like *World Café*[iv] and *Open Space Technology*[v] are free for anyone to use and are especially powerful, as they encourage the participation of everyone in the room and harness the synergy to find creative ways forward.

In contrast, when a church leadership tries to find ways forward on their own without consulting the congregation, they are limited by not knowing what their people truly feel or think. They are constrained by the existing culture, afraid to push into areas of perceived sociological resistance.

If managed well, consulting widely within your congregation has significant benefits. As church families begin to envision a new future together and form a common language to describe it, they begin building consensus around what they as a family should do about it.

Appreciative Inquiry

The tools I have mentioned are great, but they are most effective when used within a broader framework or process for change. In working with other churches, we like to facilitate conversations using a process called Appreciative Inquiry (AI),[vi] from which the principles of a conversation worth having were derived.

What we love about AI is that it is not problem focused. The traditional approach to change is to look for the problem, get to the root of it and then find a solution. However, when we look for problems, that is exactly what we find. By paying attention to problems we emphasise and amplify them.

AI suggests looking instead for what is already working in line with our goal. The reality is that in every church *something* is working that keeps people faithful and engaged—and this is the best starting point for a family conversation. We believe this also accords with Scripture, which exhorts us to focus on what is true, noble, right, pure, lovely and admirable (Philippians 4:8).

Using a workshop format, our participants are encouraged to remember their energising moments of success, and to imagine and plan for a future where this success is in evidence. As a unifying, positive energy is created, participants take with them a new sense of commitment, confidence and achievement. The outcome of the inquiry process is agreement on a series of statements that describe where the church wants to be, based on the high moments of when the church was at its best. Because the statements are grounded in real experience and history, our people know how to repeat their success.

> In every church something is already working—this is the best starting point for a family conversation

Here are just some of the assumptions of AI:

- In every society, organisation or group, something works and is worthy of our focus.

- What we focus on becomes our reality.

- We grow in the direction of the questions we ask.

- We have more confidence journeying to an unknown future when we carry forward parts of the known past.

- It is important to value differences.

- The language we use creates our reality.

When we work with churches, we take them through a five-step change process known as the five 'D's':

- **Define** the growth step you desire.

- **Discover** the best of what is in line with your goal, remembering when you did this well.

- **Dream** about what could be if you did this well in the future.

- **Design** what you will do; plan to make this dream a reality.

- **Deploy** the plan by aligning leadership, language, structure and resources to support the outcome.

The beauty of this process is that there are many creative ways to engage people in it, and it is scalable to settings great and small. It works as well for small teams as for a whole organisation. It can also be used iteratively, with each new cycle of the process building on our experiences of success and taking us closer to our dream with increasing clarity.

Sometimes the gathering will coalesce around a single plan, while other times there is sufficient support for several plans to be worked through in tandem. The important thing is that the church family leaves the workshop owning their part in the way forward without flicking all responsibility for actioning the plan/s back onto the church leadership.

We have found it very useful to term these workshop outcomes, 'experiments.' This takes the pressure off, knowing that we have the freedom to fail, and that we will simply be trying out these new ideas for an initial trial period to see if they work. Taking this approach increases enthusiasm for attempting something novel, which in turn makes it more likely that there will be a positive outcome. The reality is that if a plan is thoroughly implemented for six months, the church culture will have changed shape along the way to incorporate it.

LEADERS MUST 'BED-IN' CHANGE

Having had a church-wide family conversation about changing to grow in the direction of our dreams, what happens next is critical and it lies in the hands of our leaders. The next question is: *How will our clarified purpose as a church change what happens on Sundays?*

This is an important question because even if the scope of the change we talked about goes way beyond Sunday, for most churches the Sunday service remains our gateway event. What we elevate on Sundays when we are all together signals what is really important to us.

After the heady excitement of having been inspired with a fresh vision for our future, when we get back together on Sunday something strange is going to happen. As we find ourselves back in our familiar Sunday environment with those who did not attend the workshop, we will unconsciously want to revert to all our usual rhythms. Our old church culture will want to reassert itself. And, if we as leaders allow this to happen, the family breakthrough will seem like a mirage that quickly fades.

As leaders we have control of the schedule and of the microphone. We also have the authority to reinforce new behaviours and help extinguish unhelpful ones that work against our desired outcomes.

Following a family conversation, it is important that we do not adopt a 'business as usual' approach. We need to disrupt our regular routines, to make a large space in the Sunday service event for revisiting what was said and agreed. This is the only way to signal that this is a significant milestone that has changed the church.

Affirm those who emerged as leaders through the consultation process. Give the microphone to those who can articulate what happened. Be clear and emphatic in your endorsement of what has happened and talk about what you and others in leadership will be doing in support.

Make conversations the new normal

A family conversation in the form of a weekend Appreciative Inquiry workshop can be a momentous occasion and a watershed moment in the life of the church. It is important, however, that our conversation is not a 'one and done' event.

It is common for church leaders to see members' meetings as potential minefields where dissent and discord may erupt. When this is our fear, it suits us that they are infrequent and carefully managed, and that we limit opportunity to speak. I have no great love for the traditional church meeting either, which passes motions and resolutions that alienate dissenters, when a true conversation may have delivered a consensus outcome that everyone was happy with.

The truth is, we don't need more church meetings, but we do need more conversations about what matters. It troubles me when I hear folk who have been regulars in church for many years say at our workshops, 'This is the first time we've ever got together to talk about this stuff!' If our church is a family, we need time to talk! Conversations that take a weekend need to be judiciously employed, but smaller conversations that help us assess how and what we are doing, can and should happen often. This helps us make frequent, smaller course corrections along the journey, rather than waiting until we feel lost and need to find a way back.

Tie your conversations to your mission statement

There may already be a mission statement on your church wall, on your website or on your Sunday PowerPoint slides. If not, right after a church-wide conversation is the perfect time to formulate one. Existing statements need to be updated to reflect the outcomes of your conversation. Links between your mission statement and the concrete steps your church will be taking to fulfil its stated mission must be made explicit and reinforced week by week.

Evaluate existing church activity in light of goals

After your church-wide conversation, the existing calendar of regular church activities and usage of your facilities will simply continue as before unless someone intervenes. As a leader you need to ask, 'Is this activity still aligned with our refreshed vision of mission? Will our facilities need to be used differently or need to be made available to different people because of the conversation we have just had as a church?'

For example, will you flag away a good idea that requires your hall on Wednesday night simply because the community indoor bowls club (now down to only seven members) has been using it every Wednesday night for time immemorial? Or how about that food bank ministry which nowadays is only serving five regular customers of doubtful need without any progress in relationship, yet needs a locked room which cannot possibly be used for another purpose?

When longstanding practices need to come to an end, only a leader has the authority to have the conversations necessary for the change that is required. The people involved may even be relieved; perhaps they too have seen that what they are doing is now of little worth but didn't want to stop for fear of disappointing you!

Redirect resource and administrative support

Hopefully, your church-wide conversation ended with certain members taking charge of making things happen. However, it is very difficult for a spoke on the wheel to communicate with other spokes without going through the hub.

The church office is going to have to provide an invaluable function by helping coordinate and communicate the plans flowing out of your conversation. Were your office staff at the conversation themselves? Are they just hired hands? In any event, their job description is likely to change in light of what has just transpired! The leader needs to work this through with staff, because resentment and stonewalling can result if a member, suddenly feeling empowered by the process, drops a folder of work onto the church administrator's desk without their foreknowledge.

Stage strategic interventions

As a leader you are likely to be focusing on the big picture more than your members are. You will notice behaviour that others are missing. You are also uniquely placed in the organisation to do something about it.

As you continue to experience your church from the inside out, you will notice many inconsistencies between what people said they wanted at the workshop and their current behaviour. Your gentle intervention will be needed, but you can't go after everything at once. You will need to identify one area where a breakthrough would make the most difference and then discern what vital behaviours are needed to get there.

Identify one area where a breakthrough would make the most difference and then discern what vital behaviours are needed to get there

In their excellent book *Influencer*, the authors speak to this very question: 'You don't have to identify thousands of behaviours . . . typically one or two vital behaviours, well executed, will yield a big difference. This is true because . . . there are moments of disproportionate influence. These are times when someone's choices either lead towards great results or set up a cascade of negative behaviours that create and perpetuate problems.' [vii]

The good news is that these critical moments are easy to spot. Replay what is happening and spot the moment when a particular behaviour would have taken events down a different, more positive path—and then go after that behaviour.

Let's say for instance that at your church-wide conversation your church set as its goal 'to move from a friendly church to a church that makes friends,' yet you notice that after church, most people unmindfully spend their time in cliques, while newcomers are being shut out. Perhaps they are thinking about making friends in the world but are losing sight of those who have just walked through the church doors.

This is a moment of disproportionate influence, because if we become more mindful of opportunities to engage relationally with strangers in our church setting, isn't it likely that this mindfulness will carry over to our private worlds?

In addressing this problem with your people, you need to engage not just their minds but their emotions too. Right now, they find their current behaviour very rewarding emotionally. They love connecting with their friends. Our impulses are to meet our emotional needs, not our strategic needs. How can you make this new behaviour emotionally rewarding? You could suggest that:

- the newcomer and the person introducing them to others both get a free coffee (this would work for me!).

- rather than forsaking their regular friendship circle in order to meet strangers, those in church family could introduce themselves to newcomers and make their acquaintance together.

- to avoid the potential embarrassment of saying 'Welcome, newcomer!' (only to discover they are a regular) one could say, 'Hi, my name is _____ , I don't think we have chatted before,' and then find out how long they have been attending. Then, introduce them to some friends. You can roleplay this behaviour for the church in under one minute in a Sunday service.

- considering what can you change in your physical environment that will make doing the right thing easy. For example, if all newcomers received a free, brightly coloured folder with information about your church it would make them easier to spot!

Show off your 'bright spots'

Chip and Dan Heath in their book *Switch: How to Change Things When Change Is Hard*,[viii] propose this pathway for bedding in a new behaviour: Find someone who is doing it right and let everyone learn from them.

Is there someone who keeps an eye out for strangers and makes a point of talking to them and including them? Catch someone doing something right and commend their behaviour publicly so that everyone can see and understand what is desired. Explain the gap between this ideal behaviour and what you normally see. Help everyone understand why imitating this behaviour is strategic to the outcome you all want.

Role-model right behaviour

There are two prongs to this idea.

The first is that, as a leader, *you* need to be role-modelling the behaviour we agreed we want from everyone. Are you yourself, through the week and on Sundays, practising the behaviour you want everyone to be accountable for? Don't be afraid to honestly speak of your efforts from the front, sharing both your successes and your failures. This isn't bragging or being 'holier than thou'; it is helping to lead change. It serves as a reminder about our mission and opens the door for others to share their experiences too. You are the leader, so don't shrink from leading.

The second prong is just as powerful. If you can get your people to role-play right behaviour for themselves and each other, you will have achieved immensely more than words alone are able to do.

Here is how we help our people role-play extending an invitation to an event, be it social or formal. We begin by reiterating the helpful elements for ensuring the invitation goes as well as possible:

- Remember that success is inviting others in the power of the Holy Spirit and leaving the results to God.

- Pray!

- Reflect on what you already know about the person's circumstances right now.

- Create rapport by showing interest in the other person first.

- Invite people to join you for the event, mentioning as many of the four attractive 'F's' (friends, food, food for thought, and freedom to participate or to leave) as are appropriate.

- Don't trap people with words like 'What are you doing on Tuesday night?' Give people space to say 'no' graciously.

We then teach our people to deal with the three possible responses to their invitation—*no, maybe,* or *yes.*

Dealing with a 'No':

- Don't take it personally!

- Smile.

- Is their reason for saying 'no' something you can help them with?

- Say, 'That's okay. May I invite you again some other time?'

- End with, 'I look forward to seeing you next time.'

- Thank God for giving you the courage to ask—and count it as success!

Dealing with a 'Maybe':

- Don't assume it is just a disguised 'no.'

- Say, 'I'm very happy that you're thinking about coming!'

- Ask, 'Would you like more information to help you decide?'

- Ask, 'To help with catering, may I check back with you by (Saturday)?'

- Give them a printed invitation to remind them, if such exists.

- Thank God for giving you the courage to ask—and count it as success!

Dealing with a 'Yes':

- Be happy, but be normal.

- Tell them you will remind them closer to the time.

- Ask, 'Do you know someone who might want to come with you?'

- Give them a printed invitation to remind them, if you have one.

- Thank God for giving you the courage to ask—and count it as success!

All of this is good practical advice, but it would make little difference if our people didn't get to actually practise it until they are comfortable with it.

At our training, we set up a big bowl of white and yellow ping-pong balls. There are twice as many yellow balls as there are white. We tell them the white balls represent a 'yes,' and the yellow balls represent a 'no' or a 'maybe.' Everyone comes up and takes a ball which they keep hidden, so no-one knows what their response will be.

Then we get participants to sit at tables of six or more. Everyone imagines a scenario and role-plays making an invitation to the person to their right. That person will respond according to the colour of their ping-pong ball, but no-one is required to make it easy! As inviting is role-played around the table, everyone gets a turn and a lot of vicarious learning is going on; someone does or says something that is an 'aha!' moment for the others, the noise level rises, laughter erupts around the room and something else creeps in too—confidence. People leave the session thinking, 'I can do this!'

What we have just done is to MAWL right behaviour (Model, Assist, Watch, Leave). This kind of practical equipping lies at the heart of every movement and should be true of our church. Paul says to Timothy:

> You have heard me teach things that have been confirmed by many reliable witnesses. Now teach these truths to other trustworthy people who will be able to pass them on to others (2 Timothy 2:2).

As you read this, I hope you see the value of role-modelling and role-playing right behaviour. But can you imagine doing something like this in your Sunday morning service?

Why not try it this Sunday? This is about changing behaviour to better fulfil our mission. It is equipping the saints. It is God-honouring. Everyone is here. Why wouldn't we skip the regular stuff for one Sunday to do something like this? I believe that is exactly what a serious church would do.

Celebrate your successes

Keep the change going. Use your platform and the church's communication channels to tell the stories of change you are seeing and give feedback on what others are saying. Demonstrate in every way you can that the conversation has changed the church. Keep reinforcing that this new behaviour reflects who you now are as a church.

RIGHT BEHAVIOUR IS CAUGHT, NOT TAUGHT

Unserious churches believe that their people will somehow work out appropriate behaviour for themselves. Serious churches model right behaviour and build accountability around it.

Jesus began His ministry with a call to 'Follow me,' to watch and imitate His work. He sent out His disciples on a mission trip to put what they had learned into practice and then He debriefed with them afterwards (Luke 10:1-23). In the course of His ministry Jesus emphasised, 'you are truly my disciples if you live as I tell you to' (John 8:31) and 'you are my friends if you obey me' (John 15:14).

Paul in 1 Corinthians 11:1 says, 'Imitate me, as I imitate Christ!' He is saying, 'Watch me, do what I do, and see how I do it.'

This process of modelling and shaping right behaviour with the support and mutual accountability of the whole group has always been the model for every church that is serious about making disciples who are on a mission to change the world.

---

[i] Jacqueline M. Stavros, Cheri Torres, and David L. Cooperrider, *Conversations Worth Having: Using Appreciative Inquiry to Fuel Productive and Meaningful Engagement*, 1 edition. (Berrett-Koehler Publishers, 2018), 34–35.

[ii] Rick Warren, *The Purpose Driven Life: What on Earth Am I Here For? 40 Days of Purpose Campaign Edition*, 1st edition. (Zondervan Press, 2002).

[iii] "Redemptive Family | Love Your Neighbour," www.loveyourneighbour.nz.

[iv] "The World Cafe," *The World Cafe*, www.theworldcafe.com

[v] "Welcome to Open Space!," *OpenSpaceWorld.ORG*, www.openspaceworld.org

[vi] See Sue Annis Hammond, *The Thin Book of Appreciative Inquiry*, 3rd edition. (Thin Book Publishing, 2013).

[vii] Joseph Grenny et al., *Influencer: The New Science of Leading Change, Second Edition*, 2 edition. (McGraw-Hill Education, 2013), 35.

[viii] See chapter 2 of Chip Heath and Dan Heath, *Switch: How to Change Things When Change Is Hard*, 1st edition. (New York: Crown Business, 2010).

7

Starting a New Family

Through the pages of this book I have been sharing a vision of church as a redemptive family planted in a place as a foretaste of the Kingdom of God. At its heart is mission by its simplest definition—growing relationships and seeking a redemptive outcome. By helping everyone to be a missioner living out their purpose, we grow the church both spiritually and numerically.

My hope is that existing churches will take seriously the call to shape towards this vision. In the previous chapter I focused on what it would take to change an existing church from the inside out. However, the simplest way to form a church as a redemptive family is to start one from scratch.

If this book has resonated with you, I want to conclude with a call to consider starting (or assist in starting) a new church family on a mission in your own place with like-minded friends just as we did.

I would venture that you have read this book because you are a leader who is interested in the shape and direction of the church. You may not yet be leading a church, but perhaps you should be!

I am not suggesting that we form new churches out of protest. You may be happy in your present church but still wish to help plant another church with a clear, simple game plan.

Still, life is too short to spend it in a church with a vision that is too small to help its members live out their calling and purpose to the full. You want to be in a church that is centred in mission and is harnessing the giftings of its members for mutual discipleship. If that is not true for the church you are in, you can work for change; you can move to another church; or you can help plant a new church with these values.

YOU CAN BE A CHURCH PLANTER

By 'church planter' I mean someone who, as part of a mutually accountable team, helps establish a new church family in a place. To be a church planter you can play any role on the team—you need not be the gifted preacher or evangelist. Whatever your role, you can be the catalyst that helps bring a team together around the vision of planting a church.

Not everyone is excited by the prospect of being a church planter. If you are drawn to the adventure of planting a church that will glorify God, it is a strong indication that God has wired you to be able to deal with the ambiguities and discouragements that face every new church plant—and is perhaps prompting you to do so.

You may be attracted to the idea, yet still fear it may be too weighty a burden for you to bear. I would like to lift that burden for you by right-sizing your fears and expectations around being a church planter.

It's always the right thing to do

Bringing about a new God-glorifying community is always within the will of God.

- The Great Commission implicitly assumes establishing new faith communities throughout the world that teach, baptise and disciple. We can only reach everyone by planting churches everywhere (Matthew 28:18-20).

- The book of Acts demonstrates that new churches are the normal and necessary result of evangelism and disciple-making, and church planting was clearly central to Paul's understanding and practice of mission (Romans 15:19-20; 1 Corinthians 3:5-6).

- God grows His church by adding to local faith communities those who are saved (1 Corinthians 3:6; Acts 2:47).

- God's plan goes beyond rescuing the lost to also transforming lives, families and communities. To do this requires a local presence (Matthew 5:13-16; 13:33).

You don't need permission

Unless you choose to have denominational ties or wish to call your new faith community a name that will require permission, you don't need to be given authority by someone else to plant a church. Down the line, when your group has grown and you believe there will be benefits in doing so, you can always choose to come under the authority of a wider body.

Share your plans with everyone who may be impacted by your decision and clarify your motivation

You may not need permission, but you do want the blessing of others on your new venture. Before you begin enlisting help or drawing people away from their present church, share your plans with everyone who may be impacted by your decision, and clarify your motivation. If you intend to move away from your present church, do all you can to part on good terms—you want to begin your new venture with a good reputation.

Of course, we have to obey the law. At the point where your meeting becomes a public gathering there will be legal requirements to consider. These might include meeting health and safety requirements, having a 'Child Safe' policy and liability insurance.

You don't need to be an expert

The ideal church planter will want to grow as a disciple and take others with him/her on that journey. They will be nurturing their personal relationship with the Lord through reading Scripture, meditation, and prayer. They also need the interpersonal skills required to build a team and extend hospitality. It helps if they are thoughtful and read a lot.

To plant a church, you don't need a theology degree; you just need adventurous, God-fearing friends, a game plan, faith, and patience. You can sign up for a theological qualification if it becomes a helpful next growth step for you.

You're not too young—or too old

With every age and stage of life comes advantages as a church planter.

Younger leaders may have more energy to start something new. They are also often more culturally attuned and may consequently connect better to unchurched people generally. Of course, young leaders lack experience, will naturally make mistakes, and may sometimes lose perspective. Young leaders may also be newly married or have young children. Yet it is often young people that do start churches.

The Baptist Tabernacle in Auckland, for example, was founded by Richard Shalders, an entrepreneurial shopkeeper, at the age of thirty. Shalders had already founded Auckland's YMCA the previous year.[i]

Mount Albert Baptist Church, also in Auckland, was started by even younger entrepreneurs, Ross Penman and Harvey Turner, who were both only twenty-four at the time.[ii]

Thomas Jefcoate, a twenty-four-year-old farm labourer arrived in Christchurch from England in January 1865 to work in the Spreydon area. He began a church in a 5m x 4m sod house standing in a fifty-acre tussock paddock. From these beginnings sprang Spreydon Baptist (now Southwest Baptist Church).[iii]

What I love about these stories is that these young people were ordinary folk doing ordinary jobs who nevertheless felt called to start a church. They weren't professional preachers and they didn't have college degrees. They weren't dreaming of becoming rock stars, all they wanted was a Christian witness in their place.

My advice to a younger church planter would be to include others who are older and wiser as partners. Older people have experienced more suffering in life. They are usually better at sympathising with wounded people and providing skilful and gracious pastoral care. You can also learn from their mistakes without having to repeat them!

Go in together with friends and have fun

Your new church family will need a core of believers who share your vision and who can exercise their giftings. It really helps if you already know, like and trust each other, because this is the initial family that you are going to be inviting others to join.

Who would you ask to share this adventure with you? *Church@onetwosix* began with three committed couples. One couple was retiring from a lifelong career of pastoring and had a wealth of wisdom to share with us. The friends you gather as part of your core need not all be your peers.

The best families know how to have fun together. Don't lose your sense of adventure. You will be working with people, so it will be messy, and discouragements are inevitable—but there will be breakthrough moments too.

Think of it as an experiment

You can't fail in attempting something for God. I look at the people God has brought to us on Sunday evenings and know that most of them would not have known or cared for each other if not for us. They would not be gathered in this place to experience the Gospel in word and deed if we had not called this church into being.

Even if we were to close down tomorrow, the story of their lives has already been permanently altered. The future is in God's hands, but however long our adventure runs for, there will remain seeds that were planted and people that were raised up and came to faith, as well as deep lessons learned that led to spiritual growth and character development in all of us. I don't think God would call that a failure.

To be worthwhile, your church plant need not last forever. Rather than feeling the burden of responsibility for getting a new 'forever church' off the ground, give yourself and your team permission to think of it as an experiment or an adventure. Whatever the outcome longer-term, good is being done today.

Start small and simple

The missional model outlined in this book is very simple. It uses invitation and hospitality to draw the friends we are making in our world to come and experience fellowship at our family table with us.

There may be a message to prepare, but there is no performance to rehearse. Church will be whatever the people make it on the day. If you are not a muso, then don't have music. Wait until you find someone else to take care of it—or stream it. You likewise don't have to be a preacher.

> There may be a message to prepare, but there is no performance to rehearse

In a small group setting you will likely be teaching rather than preaching, and this role can be shared with others in your group. As the group grows there is time and opportunity for you to grow too, both in skills and in confidence. With growth will also come more available resources and a larger pool of skills and giftings to help share the load.

Don't try to copy 'regular' church. The beauty of starting something new is that you can create your own culture from scratch. Build a church with mission at its heart. Make the most of all the relational advantages of being small, in order to become a close-knit yet ever-inclusive, outward-looking family.

You don't need to call it church

There may be reasons why you don't want to call your group a church until it reaches a certain level of maturity. If 'church' is somehow a loaded term in your world, call it something else. However, you need to know that you are a church in God's eyes; you are a redemptive family on a mission together, bringing a foretaste of the Kingdom to the place where God has planted you.

You don't need to leave your present church

We know church-planters who believed that they needed to leave their church to focus all their energy and attention on their new church plant. It is true that belonging to two churches undoubtedly complicates one's life, but while leaving was the right decision for them, it may not be so for you.

For now, you may wish to retain your ties with the church you presently attend, especially if it is supportive of your efforts and you have the opportunity to feed back to them your learnings as you do something fresh. Your new work may even be an opportunity to disciple those you are already working with. Also, if your experiment lasts for a short season and reaches an end, your good relationship with your home church means you need not be cut adrift.

However, accepted wisdom is that you cannot belong to two churches at once. Having announced that you are starting a new church, many will assume that you are 'on your way out' and will begin treating you accordingly. This may be a reason not to call your newly gathered faith community a church too early.

I do, however, want to challenge the assumption that one cannot truly belong to more than one church family. *Church@onetwosix* was begun unconventionally with borrowed members who were settled in their own

> It is a fallacy that loyalty to one church family precludes loyalty to another

churches but were up for a bit of an adventure. Four years later, many of our folk still attend their 'morning church' but remain committed to this church plant, which meets Sunday evenings. This is true even for our church leaders! Contrary to popular wisdom, it appears we are willing to make more space for church in our life if we find it purposeful and meaningful.

I think it is a fallacy that loyalty to one church family precludes loyalty to another. Just as with our natural extended families, we sometimes meet with one side of the family and sometimes with the other, but we can equally enjoy being with both. Cousins on one side may have never met our cousins on the other, yet they are both legitimately and equally family to us. Expanding our circle of who is spiritual family to us does not mean that we care for anyone less.

As your new church grows, there may come a time when you do have to choose, simply because you will need to simplify your life—but leaving need not be a necessity from the outset.

Integrate your life

Instead of having to maintain separate boxes for church, family, mission and work, a new faith community starting around your own dining table is an excellent way to integrate all of life (with your family's consent, of course!)

Invited to this table could be your neighbour, work partner, flatmate and anyone else in your world with whom you have found a friendship. Instead of being constrained to a 'target audience' box, mission can be an organic process of befriending anyone God brings across your path and inviting them to experience this home-grown faith community for themselves.

One of the privileges of being in ministry with my wife Lynette was that our mission work naturally made apprentices of our children too. They have been discipled through watching and listening to us and through conversations around the table. They have also been shaped by getting to know our ministry colleagues, some of whom have been inspirational. They have seen us wrestle with ministering to difficult, awkward, broken people whom God dearly loves, and have seen when we made mistakes and when we were wise. They are ambassadors for Christ in their own world too, and now we also learn from them!

> They have seen us ministering to difficult, awkward, broken people whom God dearly loves, and have seen when we made mistakes and when we were wise

I share this to point out that having your whole family involved in the ministry happening around your table can be a precious gift. This is the kind of first-hand discipleship practised by Jesus Himself. You will also be modelling an integrated life to the next generation.

Consider co-vocational ministry

You don't need to give up the day job that you love to plant a church.

Historically, the phrase 'bi-vocational pastor' has been used to refer to a leader who served a church that was unable to compensate a pastor with a full-time salary. This pastor would work a second or third job to supplement what the church could provide, usually out of necessity rather than preference.

Often the language of 'tentmaker' (the apostle Paul's trade, described in Acts 18) has been used to define this type of church planter. However, today more church planters are choosing to operate bi-vocationally out of the conviction that this a more desirable way to plant a new church, rather than because of limited funds. In other words, it is becoming a first option, not a last resort.

For this reason, the term 'co-vocational'[iv] is a better way of describing this practice of both deeply valuing engagement and service in the marketplace and the communal living out of our mission.

Rather than giving up the natural connections to the lost that you have in your world by moving away from regular employment into a church bubble, you can instead help model to your church family how to be a disciple in the workplace.

There are other good reasons why you would choose to support yourself and serve as a volunteer in the mission:

- A volunteer model is easier to replicate.

- When someone is paid to do a job, it becomes theirs, and others are generally happy to leave them to it. Volunteers often need to share the load, making it easier for everyone to own the mission.

- The paid leader becomes a professional and a clergy-laity gap appears. If we are to be a family on a mission together where everyone's contribution is taken seriously, this gap is not helpful. 'Family' and 'professional' do not go together well.

- For your new church to pay you, it needs a twin focus — the mission and financial viability. This naturally leads to an emphasis on numbers and attracting good earners. Church can more willingly embrace the poor and marginalised without concerns about financial sustainability when everyone is a volunteer.

- Having your livelihood wrapped up in your church has the potential to cause personal angst and increases the temptation to make self-serving decisions.

Embrace a scalable model

I have suggested your home as a starting point for your new church plant, but the family model of church I have described is not just about 'house church.' There is no reason to limit the size of your church to the number that can fit in your lounge. The defining characteristic of this model of church is just that it is capable of giving expression to the church as family, not that it is very small.

At *church@onetwosix* we have structured our space and our time around belonging. We sit at tables and we encourage meaningful conversation by asking good questions. Most of our time together is dedicated to building family connection, with a focus on mutual support and accountability. We are constrained by the size of the space we presently have, but we regularly accommodate 50-60 people and it works well. So, is there an upper limit on the number of people who can truly be church family for each other?

The Dunbar number[v] (proposed by British anthropologist Robin Dunbar) is a suggested cognitive limit to the number of people with whom one can maintain stable social relationships in which an individual knows who each person is and how each person relates to every other person. That number is widely thought to be around 150.

Malcolm Gladwell, in his popular book *The Tipping Point*[vi] discusses the Dunbar number and describes the company known for the Gore-Tex brand. Through trial and error, the company discovered that once a top limit of 150 employees per building was reached, social problems began interfering with productivity. Since then, the company has designed their buildings accordingly.

Whatever the true figure, it appears there is indeed an upper limit. Should God so bless your church plant with numbers that it becomes difficult to know everyone well, it is time to plant another! Seeking to extend God's Kingdom as a family on a mission is not just a matter of growing larger, but of multiplying the number of church families reaching their world.

MAKING A START

Find your core

Think and pray about the people in your proximity that you respect and would feel privileged to plant a church with. They need not be of the same age or be at the same stage of life as you are. Teaming youthful energy with the wisdom of age can be a good thing!

Share your dream with those people. Be clear on the model of church you have in mind. Perhaps lend them this book! Also be clear on how the core team will function together. Will there be a leader? Will you operate by consensus?

The fact that you are taking the initiative does not mean that you must be the 'front person' for the new church plant. You may bring other giftings (you are already proving yourself to be a vision-caster, for instance). Let your proposed core team members know what you value about them and let them see the contribution they can make.

Adopt your place

You will want your church to gather somewhere where it can also be a blessing to its place as it grows. There are different ways you could determine where this will be. You may have been prompted to start a church because God has already laid on your heart a place you wish to serve, and you are asking your core to join you there. If you are planning to start in a home, it seems logical to adopt its locality as your place.

However, if the place you start out in is not yet decided, you may like to consider a location which is already familiar territory to one or more of your team. Local knowledge is valuable. Where would they recommend you meet? Alternatively, is there a place that already serves as a natural centre of gravity for your team? If so, discover as much about it as you can. How many churches currently serve the area? Again, where would you meet?

Gather others

Unless you have gathered a large core team, you may wish to find critical mass by inviting others to help get you off the ground. Newcomers can feel like intruders when they enter a group that feels too small and cosy. My suggested starting number is one that is too big for a single conversation group. Being able to recombine groups and move between them is a helpful dynamic for insiders and outsiders alike. In smaller groups, everyone gets a chance to contribute—and we can take turns with the awkward person who would otherwise disrupt the whole meeting. I would say nine plus is a good baseline number.

The committed core owns the venture

The committed core owns the venture. The *Love Your Neighbour* team committed to giving our church plant a go for three years before calling it a success or failure. We had to declare our intention and carry others along with us.

For those who make up your initial 'critical mass,' the bar may be lower. At the start of *church@onetwosix*, we cast vision for the need, invited others to join us on the adventure for just a year, and asked that they help replace themselves in that time. We made our gathering at a time that did not conflict with their normal church. We honoured their time-limited commitment by thanking them and giving them the freedom to leave at the end of the year.

PEGGING OUT YOUR TENT

We take a family camping holiday every year with a big 'old school' canvas tent. One thing we have learned is how important it is to get the four corners pegged out straight and true before we continue erecting the tent. Get this wrong and there will be wrinkles in the floor, the roof will sag and let the rain in, and the zip-doors won't work properly.

The four corners that you need to peg out as a church planter are the four big ideas for being a redemptive family outlined in this book. The kind of church you want to be planting is: *a family, planted in a place, on a mission, together.* These four corners will anchor the culture of your new church plant.

Let's review them one last time.:

Church as a family . . .

When we are talking about a church family centred in mission, there first has to be a family! Even friends need to be prepared to go to a deeper level with each other if they are to be mutually accountable for their personal spiritual growth and for reaching out to others.

We may assume just working on the mission will bond us as a team, but that is only true to a point. We need to truly know each other. Unless we are having conversations with each other about the things that matter most and are being real with each other about our own brokenness and need for forgiveness and healing in the corners of our lives, outsiders looking in will see proud, 'perfect' people rather than a true family of Jesus.

Practically, this means we need plenty of time to talk. This enables us to:

- discover each other's passion and giftings

- feel safe so we can be transparent about our own brokenness

- learn to trust each other so that we can be mutually accountable

- share about the people in our lives

- prioritise praying together.

We also need to be family to share the load without it feeling like an imposition. A team might keep score; a family shouldn't. Our church plant needs to be a family business where:

- everyone cares and wants to see it succeed

- everyone is a volunteer, but our reward is our inheritance at the end

- everyone does what they do best, but everyone also helps out with unpleasant chores

- everyone is thinking all the time about how we could make it better

- we deal with conflict openly and constructively.

If you are going to be inviting friends 'home' to meet your church family, they should find:

- a culture of invitation and hospitality

- that visitors and newcomers are warmly anticipated

- a group that is inclusive, welcoming, flexible

- an active, shared interest in everyone who comes

- that being with them is to experience an authentic family of Jesus.

. . . in a place

It can be tempting to ignore this corner peg and to settle for being an evangelistic church family that doesn't concern itself with place.

However, as we have seen, place gives our mission scope. God plants us in a place to be a conduit of blessing to all who live there. Caring for our place calls us to practice all of God's mission for the church, including serving society and caring for our environment. It is in our place that we will encounter the least and the marginalised, whereas in our personal bubbles we are most likely to find people just like ourselves. It is also the constancy of our focus on place that helps us be agents of transformation and a light on a hill to our neighbours.

Given that embracing our place is important, we need to deal with the fact that only some of those in our church family may actually live in the place we want to serve. How are we to think about this?

At *church@onetwosix* we stated from the outset that we are a local church that embraces our suburb of Point Chevalier. However, while a good number of our folk do indeed live in Point Chevalier, others come to us from farther afield. Here is what we do:

- While remaining missioners in our own world, we make reaching Point Chevalier our family focus. We look for ways we can support the local relationships of our members. We empower our local members by helping them help others. Does a neighbour need help sorting out the garden? We can form a team to make it happen. Does an acquaintance need a food parcel? We can help with that too.

- We create shoulder-to-shoulder opportunities to serve alongside the people of Point Chevalier. Under our 'I love Pt. Chev.' brand, we have promoted opportunities for beach-cleaning and tree-planting, painted out graffiti, and made pallet gardens for the local community centre. These were all opportunities to meet locals and grow relationships with them.

- We have had seasons of prayer-walking our suburb, praying God's blessing on the area.

- We have a sandwich board that we put out, inviting passers-by to come in for prayer.

- At church we are willing to talk about the stuff that matters to our locals, even if it feels political and makes us uncomfortable. We accompany members to their social welfare meetings. We share the concerns of our place in respect to debt and unaffordable housing and ask what we as a church can do about it.

. . . on a mission

We think of mission in terms of forming and sharing redemptive relationships, drawing others to our church family through invitation and hospitality.

What we care about is a significant determinant of who we will meet. The people who we are with at work are in our orbit because we chose that career. Our recreation of choice brings us into contact with certain others.

Likewise, when we embrace the whole mission of the church and concern ourselves with social justice and creation care, we are brought into contact with those who share our concern and those with the power to bring about change. Each of these people are loved by God. Even if we initially experience them as adversarial, our desire is to see them reconciled to God with a place at our table.

Don't assume that because the model of mission outlined in this book is simple that everyone is naturally equipped to just go out and do it.

- Familiarise your people with a Gospel outline that makes sense of your mission. This is personally clarifying for them and helps them articulate the Gospel to others.

- Keep talking about the mission. This keeps it at the forefront of people's minds. Most opportunities are lost because of a lack of mindfulness in the moment.

- Encourage the stories of encounters, whatever the outcome. Mission is about living out our faith. Ask specifics so that everyone can learn vicariously from each other.

- Train and equip your people in relationship-building and in extending an invitation.

- Create intentional opportunities to engage relationally with people in your place.

. . . together

A key understanding of church as a redemptive family is that our mission is also communal. We are not called to be lone rangers in our world, each contending alone for the Gospel. As a church we support the mission of our members in these ways:

- We have a lively expectation that our members will be engaged in mission and we involve ourselves in their story.

- We offer our members accountability, support and encouragement through small groups. Your church start-up may have just one group at first.

- We look to involve each other in the lives of the friends we are making. We seek to grow the number of Christian influencers in their lives by sharing our relationships with each other.

- We celebrate and rejoice together at every success. We share the pain and hurt too when Christ is rejected, because we are invested.

FIND A SUPPORT NETWORK

Being able to share with others in the same boat and learn from them is a huge benefit.

Love Your Neighbour is growing and supporting a 'Redemptive Family' network for church planters using this model. There are a host of resources and forums that support this simple, relational style of church. Here are some:

- *redemptivefamily.org*—support for the 'Redemptive Family' model of church.

- *wearechurch.com*—a church planting network started by Francis Chan.

- *acts29.com*—a diverse, global family of church-planters and church-planting churches.

- *3dmovements.com*—an organisation that empowers missional disciples to change the world.

- *namb.net* — the North American Mission Board, an agency that offers resources for church-planters.

- *Co-vocational Church Planting* (Facebook group) — resources, networking, and encouragement for co-vocational church planters.

- *parishcollective.org* — a global movement of Christians reimagining what it means to be the church in, with, and for the neighbourhood.

CONCLUSION

I began this book by sharing my disquiet at how church can seem to be a Sunday performance for consumers that fails to make disciples. I then told my own story to outline a simple alternative which envisages church as a redemptive family with mission at its heart and which cannot help but form disciples along the way. Rather than be a spectator, in this kind of church we are each expected to take our turn as lead player.

The model is simple and replicable and requires little resourcing. It is not dependant on staff and can be implemented by volunteers. It is scalable from a group of 10 to around 150 (a number larger than the size of most churches in New Zealand) but can easily multiply.

I have also sought to demonstrate that this model is thoroughly biblical, and that its relational form of mission finds precedent in the ministry of Jesus Himself and in the early church.

The challenge of this model is the level of transparency and accountability it requires. Its focus on relationship-building, both within the family and as the basis for mission, takes time and can't be done to schedule. But building redemptive relationships is God's plan for the church — and we risk missing our purpose if we desire that church be comfortable and convenient above all else.

When the church has clarity of purpose and shapes itself around that, gladly paying the cost, the Holy Spirit fills our sails and we begin moving forwards again. Joy returns to anaemic, washed-out spiritual lives as we start to grow. May it be so. This is my prayer for the church.

i "Our History," *Auckland Baptist Tabernacle,* www.tabernacle.org.nz/our-history

ii "Our Story," www.mabc.org.nz/our-story

iii "Spreydon's History," *SWBC - South West Baptist Church,* n.d., www.swbc.org.nz/about-us/our-history/our-history

iv "E-Book: Co-vocational Church Planting," *NAMB,* www.namb.net/send-network-blog/ebook-covocational-church-planting

v "Dunbar's Number," *Wikipedia*

vi Malcolm Gladwell, *The Tipping Point: How Little Things Can Make a Big Difference* (Boston: Back Bay Books, 2002), 91–95.

Questions for Group Discussion

Chapter 1—Out of the Kettle

1. If we tend to give the majority of our time to what is most important, what takes priority in the church you attend?

2. Do you know what your church's mission is? Is it clear what part you can play in that mission, and are you encouraged to do so?

3. Is there a sense of excitement around your church's mission, and is it bearing fruit? Do you feel like you are part of a movement?

4. Does your church demonstrate how to do mission and equip its members?

5. How would you describe your first experience of church? To what extent did coming to church feel like 'coming home?'

6. Why do you think Christians generally separate 'evangelism' from 'discipleship'? Do you think this approach has helped or hindered God's mission in your community?

Chapter 2—Only a Family can Fulfil the Church's Purpose

1. What alternatives to 'family' do we traditionally look to as our models for church?

2. In what ways has an 'epidemic of loneliness' affected your culture or community? Do you agree that 'church as family' could offer the most culturally relevant expression of church in our generation?

3. How can we foster belonging and unconditional love in our church communities?

4. How might the hospitality evident in the early church be expressed in today's culture?

5. Howard Webb writes: 'We wanted to create a model of church that was centred in mission, not just be a church that occasionally did missional things.' Which church activities do you consider missional in nature, and why?

6. Do you know people who have converted to Christianity 'at great relational cost'? How might the church be more like family in these circumstances?

7. To what extent would you consider your church to be your family?

Chapter 3—Embracing our Place

1. What would it take for a church to be truly grounded in a place?

2. What might the biblical concept of 'shalom' look like in your community?

3. How do discipleship groups based on geographical proximity have an advantage over groups based solely on natural affinity or shared common interests?

4. The author mentioned three 'roadblocks' to embracing place. What roadblocks might you or your church need to overcome in order to pledge to a local community long-term?

5. Where would you say is 'your community'? What proportion of your life is spent in that community? What could you do to increase that figure?

6. Have you ever prayer-walked your community, either alone or with others? If so, what shifted for you when you did that?

Chapter 4—Clarifying our Mission

1. What is God's ultimate mission and what is your part in it?

2. What could you do to engage more in nurturing redemptive relationships?

3. How aligned is the core purpose of your church community with God's mission? What evidence would you look for?

4. How does your church community help you live 'on mission'?

5. What steps can you take to transition to a model of mission where everybody is needed?

6. Howard writes: 'Any relationship that glorifies God by pointing to Him is redemptive.' Describe the key redemptive relationships in your life at the moment.

7. Investing in redemptive relationships takes time. What 'time-robbers' can you identify in your life? How might you rearrange your priorities to better align with God's heart for mission?

Chapter 5—Being on Mission Together

1. What barriers must you overcome so that the three pillars of culture-building can be established in your church community?

2. How might the concept of 'demonstrating belonging by behaving like a host rather than a guest' give you confidence to place trust in the people you welcome in?

3. What was your reaction to *church@onetwosix*'s use of portraits on their walls?

4. What wider community initiatives could your group join in with? What church-community collaborations have you seen that have worked well?

5. In what areas did your church community score strongest in the diagnostic checklist? What is your weakest score, and what could you do to grow in that area?

Chapter 6—Embracing Change for a Hopeful Future

1. Howard articulates three ways the church primarily glorifies God in the world. Which of these (building the church, serving society, practising creation care) resonates most strongly with you?

2. How would you describe your own style of leadership? How would it look to lead as a facilitator within a team?

3. Have you ever been part of a church-wide conversation? How could you plan for such a conversation to take place? Who could lend a hand to make it work?

4. What pre-existing aspects of your church community are working well and could best provide a starting point for a family conversation?

Chapter 7—Starting a New Family

1. Are you excited by the prospect of being a church-planter?

2. What (if any) hesitation do you have in relation to fulfilling your calling as a missioner or church-planter?

3. What encouraged you most in this chapter?

4. Consider your vision in terms of God's mission. Who would you most like to join you in your vision, and why?

5. How could you embrace place from the get-go?

6. Which of the support networks listed in this chapter seem an appropriate fit for you as you move forward?

Recommended Resources

The following resource list complements the message on this book and supports church communities to foster and build family wherever they are placed:

BOOKS

Conversations Worth Having: *Using appreciative inquiry to fuel productive and meaningful engagement,* by J Stavros, C Torres, & D Cooperrider

Family on Mission: *Integrating discipleship into the fabric of our everyday lives,* by M. & S. Breen

Faithful Presence: *Seven disciplines that shape the church for mission,* by D Fitch

God Space: *Where spiritual conversations happen naturally,* by Doug Pollock

I Once Was Lost: *What postmodern skeptics taught us about their path to Jesus,* by D. Everts & D. Schaupp

Influencer: *The new science of leading change,* by J. Grenny, K. Patterson, D. Maxfield, R. McMillan & A. Switzler

No Home Like Place: *A Christian theology of place,* by Leonard Hjalmarson

Switch: *How to change things when change is hard,* by Chip Heath & Dan Heath

The Heart of Church and Mission, by Brian Knell

The Mission of God: *Unlocking the Bible's grand narrative,* by Christopher J. H. Wright

The Search to Belong: *Rethinking intimacy, community, and small groups,* by Joseph R. Myers

Total Church: *A radical reshaping around Gospel and mission,* by T. Chester & S. Timmis

Villages Without Walls: *An exploration of the necessity of building Christian community in a post-Christian world,* by Nigel Dixon

MOBILE APPS

God Tools—a digital tract available in many languages, by *Cru.*

Prayer Atlas—an app to aid prayer walking, by *snapshot.is.*

Voke—video-based conversations to empower evangelism and apologetics, by *Cru.*

EVANGELISTIC TOOLS

The Alpha Course See: www.alpha.org

Try Praying. See: www.trypraying.org

Love Your Neighbour helps whole church families embrace their mission.

We encourage positive change in churches seeking to be more effective in mission through stories, resources, and workshop facilitation.

Find out more at: **www.loveyourneighbour.nz**

Redemptive Family Church Series

Here is an easy way to lead into a positive church-wide conversation about being a family, rooted in a place, on a mission together.

This six-week programme includes personal devotions, sermon outlines, small group study material as well as weekly surveys that provide feedback to church leadership through the series.

A workshop at the end brings your people together to agree on a practical next step to reach their desired goal.

For more information, visit **www.redemptivefamily.org**

Redemptive Family Church Planting

Inspired to plant a church? Join a growing network of likeminded people to share resources, ideas, and encouragement at **www.redemptivefamily.org**

The Inviting Workshop

Invitation lies at the heart of our church's mission and we believe anyone can be a successful inviter!

At our Inviting Workshop we address the root causes of why we fail to invite others: a faulty definition of success, our fear of social awkwardness and lack of modelling in how to do it well.

We provide a fun and practical 2.5-hour workshop for your whole church that will upskill your congregation and make invitation easy!

www.loveyourneighbour.org

Church-wide Conversations

Is it time for your church to have a conversation about things that matter most?

The Love Your Neighbour team is experienced at facilitating church-wide conversations using the Appreciative Inquiry process that will leave your people envisioned and uplifted.

Get in touch with the Love Your Neighbour team to explore the possibilities.

www.loveyourneighbour.nz

* * *

Love Your Neighbour is a faith ministry funded through donations.
To help support our work go to: www.loveyourneighbour.nz/give